Death Defying

Death Defying

Dismantling the
Execution Machinery
in 21st Century U.S.A.

PAM McALLISTER

continuum
NEW YORK · LONDON

2003

The Continuum International Publishing Group Inc
15 East 26 Street, New York, NY 10010

The Continuum International Publishing Group Ltd
The Tower Building, 11 York Road, London SE1 7NX

Printed in the United States of America

Library of Congress Cataloging in Publication Data

McAllister, Pam.
Death defying : dismantling the execution machinery in 21st century
U.S.A. / Pam McAllister.
p.   cm.
Includes bibliographical references and index.
ISBN 0-8264-1463-X
1. Capital punishment—United States.   I. Title.
HV8699.U5M38   2003
364.66′0973—dc21   2003014548

This book is dedicated to the Reverend Dr. Constance M. Baugh, my friend and sister in the faith, whose dedication to the voiceless and marginalized, willingness to speak truth to power, and fierce passion for justice have profoundly touched my life and inspired me.

This book is also dedicated to Ross Byrd, whom I have never met. His father, a black man, was tied to the back of a pickup truck and dragged through the streets of Jasper, Texas, to his death. Two of the white men found guilty of this crime were sentenced to die. Ross Byrd is fighting for their lives. I am in awe of his merciful heart, his moral strength, and his refusal to give in to revenge.

It seems to me that Connie Baugh and Ross Byrd live their lives in ways that exemplify the prayer of Saint Francis—"where there is hatred, let me sow love; where there is injury, pardon."

❧ Contents ❧

❧ Acknowledgments ❧

It is always easy to feel isolated when writing a book, but *Death Defying*, with its bleak and unforgiving subject matter, was especially challenging. For over two years, I cried and raged my way through stories of horrendous crimes, wasted lives, and bureaucratic brutality. Ironically, I was sometimes paralyzed by feelings of desperate urgency. I wanted a clarion call—JUST STOP THE KILLING!—to be enough: writing this book is my concession to the merit and reality of the struggle's long haul.

To stay focused and faithful to the writing of this book, I've had to call on resources that are life-affirming. I've needed my family and friends; my beloved cat-companion, Sophia; my church community; my music-making; and New York City's carnival of concerts, movies, and plays, bookstores, libraries, and cafés; the you're-not-alone-in-this-crazy-world reality checks of WBAI-Pacifica Radio and National Public Radio; and, of course, Brooklyn's Prospect Park and Botanic Garden—places that feed my soul with their seasons of beauty.

I am most grateful to my family for their love and support, especially my parents, Helen and Arden McAllister, who have grounded me in *agape*-love since childhood, and set an example of courageous action with their lives. I am also grateful for the love, friendship, deep connection, mutual respect, and encouragement of my sister Lois McAllister Baum and of her husband, my "bro," Greg.

I owe a dept of gratitude to my friend Joyce Pyle and to my mother (again). They both faithfully clipped their newspapers for me, calling to my attention items pertaining to death penalty law, capital cases, and news about the prison industry and the criminal justice system. In addition, Joyce read many parts of this book aloud to me, listened to my daily reflections about the writing process, and gave moral support in ways great and small.

Connie Baugh helped me talk through my earliest thoughts about this project. Later, she lent me many books from her personal criminal justice library. When those books were temporarily lost in the mail, Mary-Elizabeth Fitzgerald retrieved them and brought them to me. I am also grateful to Tom Lawrence, Debbie Cordonnier, David Dyson, and Elizabeth Alexander for sharing their resources and ideas with me and for giving me encouragement.

Cynthia Powell, Carol Scott, Rich Schrader, and (again) my sister Lois read the first draft of my manuscript with care and took the time to make detailed notes and to discuss their reactions with me. Their constructive feedback greatly strengthened the book.

I am grateful to Nelson Howe for his long hours of careful listening, for sharing laughter and tears, and for helping me trust the power of my gifts.

When my computer crashed just before I was ready to print the final draft, Mary Savage and the women of Stone Soup Brooklyn Community Storytellers fed me strawberries and wiped away my tears, and Susan Bowen brought my computer back to life with her calm charm.

Finally, I am grateful to my editor, Evander Lomke, for believing in this book from the beginning, for gallantly sparing me many dreaded elevator rides, and for putting all the pieces together with care and attention to detail. It is a true joy to work with him.

PAM McALLISTER
June, 2003

✍ Death Defying Steps ❧
of Extraordinary Optimism

I had breakfast with my friend Nancy at a sunny cafe on the morning after the death penalty was reinstated in New York State, in 1995. The city was full of harsh rush hour sounds—honking horns, grinding garbage trucks, yelling school children, and businesspeople calling "taxi! taxi!"

Everything seemed too loud that morning, as the city shook itself awake. We had all been sleeping, I thought, not paying attention. "What the hell happened?" Nancy asked. Comfortably dozing in our politically liberal Brooklyn neighborhood, we had stopped paying attention, and now we were stunned. New York would have a death penalty again. I ordered another cup of coffee and silently made a pledge to do something about the situation, now that I was awake. This book is the product of that morning's pledge.

This book is for those who have not fallen asleep, but have remained vigilant and active, defying death by working for the healing of our broken world. Seasoned organizers, who know more than I ever will about working against capital punishment, might find here some fuel to bolster sagging spirits as well as some new ideas.

This book is also for those who, like me, mean well but get easily distracted, sidetracked, or lulled into indulgent inactivity by the assumption that society is slowly progressing away from a system of revenge and retribution toward a system of reconciliation and restoration.

Concerned couch potatoes, who want to make a difference but don't know where to start, will find words intended to inspire and energize.

This is a book for people living in a post-9/11 world—all of us too busy and with too much on our plates to take lots of time to think about capital punishment. And why should we? There is so much to do, so many challenges to face. Our landscape keeps changing. Towers crumble and desert winds blow. Everything seems at once both fragile and harsh. Name a concern and people of conscience are grappling with it—racism and sexism (institutional and personal), poverty, civil liberties, the environment, animal rights, hunger, militarism, homelessness, corporate greed and corruption, the war on terrorism, gun control, and—the list is overwhelming. Where, in the midst of all this, is there time or energy to care for death row inmates, people so far on the fringe of our awareness they are all but invisible? Indeed, it is fair to say that it would be fine with most people if the condemned stayed that way. Condemned and out of sight. We have acquiesced in their banishment from society. "Die," we've said, or permitted our justice system to say for us. Of all the things to care about, this one is at the bottom of most lists. Death row inmates are losers anyway, with scruffy, poor, wasted lives. Good riddance.

This book is a meditation on reasons why those of us—so busy with other worthy causes—need to care about and work against capital punishment.

As it happens, the death penalty abolition movement is a movement with momentum. It is not a losing battle, especially these days when the Supreme Court is cautiously chipping away at the broken old system and when ordinary citizens are stunned at, and perplexed by, the alarming number of death row inmates who have been found innocent after all, and freed.

Those of us who oppose capital punishment in the United States find ourselves walking a tightrope that stretches from cynicism to idealism. We take a bold step toward the hopeful end of the continuum, (say, for example, when the Supreme Court rules that it is unconstitutional to execute the mentally retarded) only to stumble back toward despair (when, within days of the new ruling, Texas decision-makers determine that the mentally retarded man they had intended to execute is—surprise! surprise!—not really retarded after all).

The big push in the capital punishment abolition movement is toward a moratorium. More and more Americans are willing to stay the executioner's hand, push the pause button on the machinery of death, long enough to take a second look and fix what is broken. We look with alarm at the growing number of condemned people being exonerated and freed from death row and wonder, with increasing dismay, not only how they will manage to put their lives back together, but where the culprits are who really committed the crimes.

Abolitionist hopes are high that a moratorium will bring the end of capital punishment in the United States. But we've been there, done that. We had a moratorium midway through the 20th century. It didn't last. Soon, we were back at it, with renewed bloodlust, stuffing men and women into cages to wait for death. This time, we have got to change heads and hearts as well as rules. This time, as the rules change, we must change too. This is our work.

Those of us who dare to oppose capital punishment in the 21st century must be willing to take death defying steps of extraordinary optimism:

death defying—a term generally associated with risky, high-stakes shocks and thrills, but here meaning literally to defy the "eye for an eye" culture of capital punishment

steps—not leaps and bounds, extreme feats, spectacular stunts or tricky maneuvers, just steps, as in "take one step at a time," determined, deliberate, courageous, faithful, and firm

extraordinary optimism—the net that stretches beneath the tightrope, which catches us each time we slip and begin to fall into cynicism or despair, (and, alas, we do slip)

One of my favorite political cartoons depicts a large crowd of worried people looking straight ahead, as if they don't see each other. Over each head is a thought-bubble with the words, I'M JUST ONE PERSON. WHAT CAN I DO? This book is my attempt to redraw that cartoon, to erase the lines of the implied collective shrug, to redraw the eyes of the cartoon people so that they stop looking straight ahead and start looking around. It is my attempt to rewrite the sentence, I'M JUST ONE PERSON and pen in the rallying cry, LOOK HOW MANY OF US THERE ARE! TOGETHER, WE CAN CHANGE THE WORLD!

⤳ 1 ⤳

The Sad and Sordid History
of Capital Punishment

📖 *The Five Chinese Brothers* by Claire Huchet Bishop

In this children's story, popular since its publication in 1938, a Chinese man is wrongfully convicted of murder and sentenced to die. Fortunately, he has four loyal and gifted brothers who look just like him. Throughout the story, the brothers use their gifts to foil the executioner.

Condemned to be beheaded, the first brother is granted permission to go and bid his mother good-bye, but the brother with an iron neck returns in his place.

When this brother proves invincible against the executioner's sword, the crowd gets angry and demands a death by drowning. The brother whose legs stretch, stealthily slips into place. When he is thrown overboard, he simply stretches his legs to the bottom of the sea and keeps his smiling face high and dry.

And so the story goes, until five methods of execution fail and the judge concludes, "We have tried to get rid of you in every possible way and somehow it cannot be done. It must be that you are innocent." The five Chinese brothers go home to their mother and live happily for many years.

Which Crimes Fit *This* Punishment?

From antiquity through most of the 20th century, people were executed for a wide range of behaviors. In the 18th century B.C.E., King Hammurabi of Babylon developed one of the earliest known code of laws. In it, twenty-five crimes were classified as capital offenses, including sorcery and the fraudulent sale of beer.

Draco, a lawmaker in 7th century B.C.E. Athens, formulated a code which made almost any offense, from the most serious to the most frivolous, punishable by death. Draco's name lives on in the modern word "draconian," which means something extremely harsh or cruel. For a time in Greece, one could be sentenced to death for being lazy.

Things were not much better in Rome, where the Law of the XII Tablets made it a capital offense to disturb the peace at night—if you were of a low class. Slaves were bound by a stricter code than free people. Juveniles received lighter punishments than adults.

In the Hebrew Scripture's book of Leviticus, both the victims and the perpetrators of sexual crimes were condemned to death.

Leviticus 20:10—If a man commits adultery with the wife of his neighbor, both the adulterer and the adulteress shall be put to death.

Leviticus 20:13—If a man lies with a male as with a woman, both of them have committed an abomination; they shall be put to death.

Leviticus 21:9—When the daughter of a priest profanes herself through prostitution, she profanes her father; she shall be burned to death.

Deuteronomy 22:23–25—If there is a young woman, a virgin already engaged to be married, and a man meets her in the town and lies with her, you shall bring both of them to the gate of that town and stone them to death, the young woman because she did not cry for help in the town and the man because he violated his neighbor's wife. So you shall purge the evil from your midst. But if the man meets the engaged woman in the open country, and the man seizes her and lies with her, then only the man who lay with her shall die.

Also according to the Hebrew Scripture, blasphemy, cursing, and disobeying one's parents are capital offenses, as is murder.

Leviticus 20:9—All who curse father or mother shall be put to death.

Leviticus 24:16—One who blasphemes the name of the Lord shall be put to death; the whole congregation shall stone the blasphemer. Aliens as well as citizens, when they blaspheme the Name, shall be put to death.

Leviticus 24:17—One who kills a human being shall be put to death.

Deuteronomy 21:18–21—If someone has a stubborn and rebellious son who will not obey his father and mother, who does not heed them when they discipline him, then his father and his mother shall take hold of him and bring him out to the elders of his town at the gate of that place. They shall say to the elders of his town, "This son of ours is stubborn and rebellious. He will not obey us. He is a glutton and a drunkard." Then all the men of the town shall stone him to death. So you shall purge the evil from your midst; and all Israel will hear and be afraid.

Throughout Europe, during the medieval period, both early and late, capital punishment was an unlucky fact of life, the risk one took for being alive. In the 13th century, the Roman Catholic Church instituted the Inquisition to combat heresy. For the next four hundred years, Inquisitors made quick work of trials and used various means of torture to execute Jews, pagans, and church reformers (later, Protestants) who refused to convert to Catholicism, and others, including free-thinkers, healers, midwives, and, as always, the poor and the mentally ill.

During this time, simply being born female could be a capital offense, and thousands of women (especially those who were unmarried or widowed), girls, and female animals were put to death in accordance with a text titled the *Malleus Maleficarum* (The Hammer of Witches). Written by two monks and published in 1484 with the official blessing of Pope Innocent VIII, this witch-hunter's manual was reproduced on the newly invented printing press and widely distributed to the literate, powerful, and predominantly male elite. In it, they read such statements as "All witchcraft comes from carnal lust, which is in women insatiable," and "Woman is a wheedling and secret enemy, she is a liar by nature."

Then, as now, the death penalty was big business. It meant jobs. In France, a laborer could be paid forty-eight francs for boiling a "heretic" in oil; in England, boiling the condemned was worth a shilling. Scrubbing the kettle after the execution was only worth two pence.

During his reign in England (1509–47), Henry VIII made liberal use of capital punishment. Several of his wives were executed, as were Sir Thomas More (martyred on a charge of high treason) and over seventy thousand other men, women, and children for a range of offenses.

In Shakespeare's day, the severed heads of traitors were displayed at the entrance to London Bridge. Parboiled and dipped in tar, they could

Execution of Protestants in the Netherlands during the Reformation era

last for years. Tyburn, a permanent gallows, was erected in 1571. Verse 1 of Psalm 51 ("Have mercy on me, O God, according to your steadfast love; according to your abundant mercy, blot out my transgressions") was dubbed the "neck verse." Reciting it could save one's neck from the noose—though it was good for one time only.

There is a story of one woman, Anne Turner, who was hanged at Tyburn in November, 1615. Before being found guilty of participating in a murder plot, Turner had invented yellow-starch for the stiff wide ruffs that were in fashion at the time. When she went to her death wearing a yellow ruff and matching cuffs, however, yellow starch suddenly went out of vogue.

England's list of crimes punishable by death numbered two hundred in the 1600s. The "Bloody Code" expanded with time. By 1780, the list of capital offenses had grown to 350 and was used throughout most of the British colonies.

In the New World's northern colonies, crimes against morality were big on the catalog of capital offenses. In Connecticut, Massachusetts, and New Hampshire, offenders could be sentenced to death for the crimes of blasphemy, idolatry, sodomy, and bestiality. In New York, one could be hanged for adultery as well as piracy and perjury. In 1701, Esther Rodgers was hanged for infanticide in Boston before an estimated crowd of four or five thousand onlookers.

The southern colonies used capital punishment more for property offenses. In Virginia it was possible to be sentenced to death for smuggling tobacco, stealing a hog, or receiving a stolen horse. In South Carolina one could die for burning the timber intended for house frames.

Some offenses were labeled capital only if committed by Africans, either enslaved or free. In South Carolina a black person caught destroying grain or certain goods could be sentenced to death in the mid-1700s. In Georgia, it was a capital offense for a slave to strike a white person hard enough to cause a bruise. In Virginia, enslaved Africans could get the death penalty merely for preparing or administering medicine. When Paul Revere made his famous ride from Boston to Lexington in 1775, he rode past the body of a slave named Mark who had been hanged for poisoning his "master."

An anti-death penalty essay by the Italian thinker Cesare Beccaria, though deemed forbidden reading by the Catholic Church, caused a stir throughout Europe and the colonies from the time of its publication in 1764. After the Revolutionary War, Beccaria's essay inspired some to join with the Quakers and others to call for the abolition of the death penalty in the young nation. The list of capital offenses remained long, however, especially in the southern states. Until the Civil War, it was possible to be put to death in the United States for sodomy, forgery, horse-stealing, rape, arson, conspiring in a slave revolt, and aiding runaway slaves.

The largest mass execution in United States history took place on the day after Christmas, in 1862, when thirty-eight people were hanged in Mankato, Minnesota. Over three hundred people of the Dakota Nation had been tried without benefit of legal representation and sentenced to death by a military court for their part in an uprising against white settlers. The death sentences were sent to President Lincoln for review. He was warned that leniency for the condemned Native Americans might result in their "indiscriminate massacre." But another voice, that of Bishop Henry Whipple, head of the Minnesota Episcopal Church, urged Lincoln to "examine the causes which have brought this bloodshed" and to show mercy. In the end, the president commuted all but thirty-eight of the sentences.

Another mass hanging made history in 1917, when nineteen black soldiers were executed on the banks of Salado Creek in Texas. Frustrated by weeks of enduring racial slurs, segregation, and police harassment, the soldiers retaliated when two white Houston police officers beat two black soldiers, killing one. In the end, fifteen white people died in the riot. Over sixty black soldiers were tried and found guilty of mutiny and murder or desertion. Nineteen were sentenced to death. There was no appeal process. *Camp Logan*, a 1989 play by Celeste Walker dramatizing the mass execution, has brought this obscure history to light in recent years.

During the Civil War (1861–65), in an effort to curb the enthusiasm of local "hanging judges," elected officials began transferring authority over executions to the state level of government. While states took on the official task of sanctioning executions, lynching—the extralegal execution of an accused person by a mob—continued to be used by the white population to terrorize and control African Americans. When lynching subsided in the 1930s, the number of legal executions rose.

The last public hanging in the United States took place in 1936 in Owensboro, Kentucky, when Rainey Bethea, a 22-year-old black man, was executed for raping a white woman. Between ten and twenty thousand white spectators attended, dressed in their Sunday best. Many bought hot dogs and drinks from busy vendors who had set up near the gallows. They jeered the condemned man, who prayed as the hood was put over his head. The jeering continued until the trap was sprung, then people rushed to the swinging body to tear off pieces of the death hood for souvenirs. The national press condemned the "callous, carnival spirit" of the execution spectators, and a shocked nation learned the limits of what it could tolerate in the name of justice.

After that, throughout the United States, the list of capital offenses narrowed, and executions moved from the public arena to the jail yard and then, deeper into the interior, to the death chamber.

The Global Shift Away from Capital Punishment

Although the 20th century saw world wars, systematic slaughter of targeted populations, and the development of weapons of mass destruction, it was also a century when the nations of the world struggled to establish international standards of action. In 1948, the United Nations adopted a Universal Declaration of Human Rights, which proclaimed that every individual was due protection from deprivation of life.

Over the years, the United Nations has proposed various protocols and safeguards, seeking to limit the death penalty or abolish it. These efforts have continued into the 21st century. In April, 2001, the United Nations Commission on Human Rights approved a European Union motion for a worldwide moratorium on capital punishment.

Since the passage of the Universal Declaration of Human Rights, a majority of nations have either abandoned the tradition of execution as barbaric or have at least significantly narrowed the list of capital offenses. According to the Rome-based anti-death penalty organization Hands Off Cain (named after the biblical character who killed his brother but was protected by God), worldwide, an estimated ninety-eight percent of all executions are implemented under dictatorial regimes. Indeed, the United States is one of the very few nations with a representative government which still uses the death penalty, and the only one where the laws regarding its implementation are not uniform throughout the nation but vary widely in different parts of the country.

The first nation to end capital punishment was Venezuela in the mid-1800s. Most other Central and South American countries followed suit. Germany, Austria and Italy abolished the death penalty right after World War II. Great Britain permanently ended executions in 1969. France stopped using the guillotine in 1977 and ended capital punishment four years later.

The Council of Europe has made abolition of the death penalty a condition of membership since 1994. The countries of Eastern Europe, having moved away from communism toward democracy, have likewise abandoned the use of capital punishment. Canada, Australia, and New Zealand renounced it. South Africa was extravagant in its use of executions until 1995 when, under the government of Nelson Mandela, it too abolished capital punishment.

The death penalty has become a diplomatic encumbrance for negotiators, as more countries refuse to extradite suspected murderers or accused terrorists to the United States, fearing the accused will be executed if found guilty. In 2001, when President George W. Bush toured Europe, he was met by demonstrators in several cities, including Madrid, where thousands chanted, "Bush assassin"—a direct reference to his enthusiastic endorsement of capital punishment.

❖ *Right now, no other issue is pushing the United States further apart from its allies and the growing consensus of international law than the death penalty. The costs to the U.S. in terms of international stature and vital cooperation from other countries are substantial.*

By defying international agreements and turning a deaf ear to the entreaties of its friends, the U.S. is increasingly positioning itself as a human rights violator on this issue. By executing juvenile offenders and the mentally ill; by executing citizens from other countries who were not afforded the simple protections U.S. citizens routinely expect abroad; and by ignoring international norms against expanding the death penalty, the U.S. is showing disrespect for international human rights law both at home and abroad.

~RICHARD C. DIETER

The lone Western democracy in the lineup of the top ten nations to condone government-sponsored executions, the United States takes its place beside China, Saddam Hussein's Iraq, the Congo, Iran, Egypt, Belarus, Taiwan, Saudi Arabia, and Singapore.

Worldwide, most executions are carried out in China, where the list of capital offenses is long—with over sixty crimes punishable by death. The judges there are not required to have legal training, but they sentence thousands to death each year for a range of crimes, including bribery, drug trafficking, stealing diesel fuel, and tax evasion. A conviction can be handed down just days after an arrest. Appeals happen fast in China, if they happen at all. An execution—usually a gunshot to the back of the head—is normally carried out within an hour after a sentence is confirmed. It is believed that the vital organs of the executed are then "harvested" for use in medical transplants.

In Japan, executions are rare. What makes that nation's system unique is that the condemned and their families are not told the execution date beforehand. Prisoners live daily with the knowledge that, any step in the hallway can be the one that brings word of their impending deaths. Given only moments to write a letter or receive last rites, a handful of inmates are gathered together and led to the gallows—generally around year's end or in early spring—to be hanged. Their families are informed after the fact.

It is said that, in Saudi Arabia, public execution is a fine art. The condemned kneel in the dirt—perhaps accused of theft or rape—where they are beheaded with a sword. This punishment may actually be preferable to "cross amputation"—the chopping off of the right hand and the left foot.

In Afghanistan, under the Taliban, it was traditional for the father of the victim to take the role of executioner.

In Iraq, under the demented but predictable Saddam Hussein, it is said that women were hanged on Tuesdays in Baghdad.

The legal system of Pakistan made international news in 2002 for its use of *hudood*—a code of laws based on the Koran, that mandates the punishment of death for all forms of adultery, "whether the offense is committed with or without the consent of the parties." One case, reported in the *New York Times* in May of that year, involved a woman named Zafran Bibi, who was convicted of adultery after she accused a man of rape. With a newborn baby in her arms and a husband serving a long prison sentence, there was no doubt that she had had sex outside the bounds of her marriage. In order to prove rape, however, she would have had to find four males, all Muslims and of upright character, to testify that they had witnessed the rape. Failing that, Zafran Bibi was sentenced to death by stoning.

In July 2002, in Multan, Pakistan, a 48-year-old man, previously found to be mentally ill, was stoned to death by an estimated crowd of almost three hundred for the crime of blasphemy. He had been found writing his own name in copies of the Koran in place of the name of the Prophet Mohammed.

In northern Nigeria that same year, Safiya Hussaini, who had given birth to a baby outside of wedlock, was found guilty of committing adultery and sentenced to death by stoning. Her case was publicized in the *New York Times* magazine, which quoted the attorney general of Sokoto State as saying he would be happy to cast the first stone—a moderate-sized one, the size of a fist, in accordance with *Shariah*, Islamic law. Perhaps because of international outrage, Safiya Hussaini was granted an acquittal in a Muslim appeals court. Several months later, Amnesty International reported that another woman in Katsina State had been sentenced to death by stoning. And so goes the situation in Nigeria.

This is our world at the dawning of the 21st century.

Crimes of the Famously Executed

Defying the powers-that-be, in one way or another, seems to be the crime of those most famously sentenced to death. The Greek philoso-

Jesus as a suffering savior, crucified on a tree-of-life, a symbol of triumph over death itself. © Julie Lonneman

Jesus as one with the world's starving, screams in agony in *The Tortured Christ*, sculpture by Brazilian artist Guido Rocha, 1975. Photo by John Taylor, courtesy of the World Council of Churches

pher Socrates, mentor of Plato, argued that the good life is one illuminated by reason, but his passion for truth offended the wrong people. He was permitted the option of killing himself with hemlock, after he was found guilty of "impiety" and condemned to death in 399 B.C.E.

Jesus of Nazareth, ca.33 C.E., proved a threat, both to the Roman Empire that occupied Palestine and to the Jewish authorities of Jerusalem. He was condemned to death by Pontius Pilate, the Roman governor, and crucified. His execution is the basis of untold numbers of songs, symphonies, paintings, statues, legends, poems, rituals, dances. Passion plays, first performed in medieval times, are reenactments of his trial, condemnation, and death by crucifixion. The cross, once an instrument of torture and execution used throughout the Roman Empire to punish everything from theft to sedition, is today the most commonly recognized symbol of the Christian religion. It is often gold-plated in church sanctuaries, or prettily dangling from an earlobe or a necklace-chain, or tattooed in blue ink on a well-muscled upper arm.

Many of the followers of Jesus were also sentenced to death, including the fisherman Peter (crucified upside down in Rome) and Stephen (stoned to death). Paul-of-Tarsus, who had once ruthlessly persecuted the apostles and other believers and had witnessed (and presumably endorsed if not cheered) Stephen's execution, had a revelation that changed his point of view. He became a staunch advocate of the Jesus movement, and was, in turn, executed in Rome himself after two years of house arrest.

On February 14, 270, a priest named Valentine was beheaded. He had been performing secret wedding ceremonies for young soldiers and their sweethearts, defying Emperor Claudius II's rule forbidding such unions. He had also refused to worship Roman gods. He was arrested and sent to prison where he worked to alleviate the suffering of other inmates, until he was executed. Eventually, the Roman empire adapted Christianity, and, in 496, officially declared February 14th St. Valentine's Day.

Jan Huss, a Czech national hero and pre-Reformation challenger of the Roman Catholic Church, fought for reform and was arrested, tried, and burned at the stake as a heretic in 1415 after valiantly defending his ideas at the Council of Constance.

Joan of Arc, burned at the stake in 1431, was another who offended both church and state. She was tried for heresy by French clerics who

Jan Huss, burned at the stake

sympathized with the English as the two countries approached the end of the Hundred Years' War.

In 1618, Sir Walter Raleigh was beheaded at the order of James I. An adventurer and poet, he had been a favorite of Queen Elizabeth, but the tides shifted. He spent more than a dozen years in the Tower of London and was set free for two years before he was led to the scaffold on a charge of high treason. Eyeing the ax, he supposedly proclaimed, "Tis a sharp remedy, but a sure cure for all ills."

Mary Dyer, not as famous as she ought to be, was executed in the struggle for religious freedom in the New World. In the mid-1650s, Quakers were outlawed in Boston. If caught, they could be stripped, whipped, mutilated, and branded, or executed and their books burned. In 1659, Dyer and two Quaker friends made the decision to test the law. Her two friends were hanged, and then the noose was put around Dyer's throat. The official in charge, however, stopped the process and warned Dyer to get out of the colony. She went home, only to return carrying her own burial shroud. She was hanged on Boston Common the next morning, but not before she managed to shout out a partial statement, "My life not availeth me in comparison to the liberty of the truth. . . ." News of Dyer's death disturbed Charles II, who pledged to put an end to the intolerant theocracy of the Puritans. Today in Boston, there is a statue of Mary Dyer bearing the legend, "Witness of religious freedom, hanged on Boston Common 1660."

Across the ocean, Marie Antoinette, the epitome of decadence, joined the ranks of the famously executed. She was the pampered queen of France, famous for answering a starving population's cry for bread with the taunt, "Then, let them eat cake!" When the French Revolution erupted she was imprisoned, then guillotined in October, 1793.

In the days before the U.S. Civil War, those who organized armed struggle against slavery were tried and executed, including Denmark Vesey in 1822 and the vision-inspired Nat Turner, hanged after the failure of his rebellion in 1831. In 1859, two years before the outbreak of the Civil War, John Brown seized the government arsenal at Harper's Ferry, Virginia, hoping for the slave insurrection he had been fostering. Instead, he was captured, tried for treason, and hanged. He used his last words to warn of the bloodshed to come.

Like the others on this list, Joe Hill, the Swedish-American labor organizer and songwriter, offended powerful enemies. When he was accused of murder in the state of Utah, on what many believed were trumped-up charges, people protested across the country. President Woodrow Wilson intervened, but failed to stop the death sentence. The day before he was executed by firing squad on November 19, 1915, Hill sent a wire to a fellow labor organizer with the admonition, "Don't waste time mourning. Organize!" In Chicago, 30,000 sympathizers marched in a funeral procession for him, fiercely promising that their martyr would be remembered as "the man who never died."

Nicola Sacco, a shoemaker, and Bartolomeo Vanzetti, a fish peddler, both immigrants and anarchists, became the focal point of impassioned political activists who were convinced that the murder charges brought against the two men were bogus and politically motivated. In a memoir entitled *The Never-Ending Wrong*, about her involvement in trying to prevent the executions, Pulitzer Prize-winner Katherine Anne Porter wrote, "They were put to death in the electric chair at Charlestown Prison at midnight on the 23rd of August, 1927, a desolate dark midnight, a night for perpetual remembrance and mourning. I was one of the many hundreds who stood in anxious vigil watching the light in the prison tower, which we had been told would fail at the moment of death; it was a moment of strange heartbreak."

Dietrich Bonhoeffer was a Lutheran pastor and theologian during Adolf Hitler's rise to power. He wrote extensively about Christianity in a secular world and took a radical stand for theological humanism. His anti-Nazi activities in the Resistance led to his arrest, imprisonment, and, in 1945, his execution at the Flossenbur concentration camp, tragically close to the end of the war.

Julius and Ethel Rosenberg should also be on a list of famously executed people. Indicted for treason and accused of being members of a Soviet spy ring, Julius, an electrical engineer, and Ethel, the mother of two small boys, died in the electric chair at Sing Sing prison in Ossining, New York, in 1953. Their case became an international cause célèbre, many people believing that they were innocent or that the information they were alleged to have passed on was not of great significance.

Neither famously executed nor currently on death row (as I write, a new sentencing trial is pending), Mumia Abu-Jamal is included as one who was condemned to death for what many believe were political reasons, and was imprisoned on death row for almost two decades. At the time of his arrest for the murder of a white police officer, Abu-Jamal was well known in Philadelphia as an award-winning print and broadcast journalist who was publicly critical of the city's police department. A former Black Panther, Abu-Jamal had earned both praise and condemnation as the "voice of the voiceless" and the President of the Philadelphia Association of Black Journalists, when *Philadelphia* magazine named him "one of the people to watch in 1981." Ironically, in December of that year, the world indeed watched as the controversial journalist was arrested for murder. The next year he was sentenced to death in a trial riddled with inconsistences. During his subsequent years on Pennsylvania's death row, a movement arose to call for a new trial, and Abu-Jamal became the catalyst for an international crusade against capital punishment.

Finally, there is Joseph Paul Jernigan. Not famous before his death, he became the "most intimately known body in the world" after his execution in Huntsville, Texas, on August 4, 1993. He and an accomplice, both desperate for money and high on drugs, had murdered an elderly witness after a burglary-gone-bad. In prison, Jernigan started a chapter of Alcoholics Anonymous for death row inmates, wrote long, reflective letters, and agreed to donate his body to medical science as a gesture of atonement for his crime. Because he died healthy and on a schedule, his corpse was handled according to the scientists' exact specifications. Ultimately, his body was cut into 1,877 slices. Each cross-section was then digitally photographed. When these photos were collated, three-dimensional-imaging technology was applied, and Jernigan was turned into the Visible Human Male and haled as "the most accurate human anatomical model ever seen." According to an article in the *New Yorker*, officials at the National Library of Medicine, with hindsight, tried to protect the donor's anonymity, but the executed man's identity had been easily deduced by reporters. Today, Jernigan lives on as the Visible Human Male, accessible on thousands of Web sites.

Not for Humans Only

One of the most bizarre aspects of the history of capital punishment is its use against animals. The Bible lists specific instances in which animals are to be put to death for committing crimes. Leviticus 20:15–16 orders death for any animal used in a sex act with a human. Animals were also condemned for causing the death of a human.

Exodus 21:28–29—When an ox gores a man or a woman to death, the ox shall be stoned, and its flesh shall not be eaten; but the owner of the ox shall not be liable. If the ox has been accustomed to gore in the past, and its owner has been warned but has not restrained it, and it kills a man or a woman, the ox shall be stoned, and its owner also shall be put to death.

In *The Laws*, Plato (ca. 427–347 B.C.E.) outlined his concept of the ideal state, which included this decree:

> If a beast of burden or any other animal shall kill anyone, except it
> be while the animal is competing in one of the public games, the

relations of the deceased shall prosecute the animal for murder; the judges shall be such overseers of the public lands as the kinsman of the deceased may appoint; and the animal, if found guilty, shall be put to death and cast beyond the boundaries of the country.

Aristophanes (ca. 450–385 B.C.E.) satirized the Athenian love of litigation and their trials (which usually had five hundred or more jurors!) in *Wasps*, a play in which a dog is tried for stealing a piece of cheese.

Today in the United States, pit bulls and other animals who have committed acts of violence against humans are dispatched to a sterile death without benefit of trial, but in other times and places, animals have been sentenced to death with great pageantry. In 1386, at Falaise in Normandy (now, northwest France), a sow was found guilty of mutilating a boy and was condemned to be hanged. The convicted pig was dressed in a vest, gloves and britches, and a human mask was placed on her head on her way to the gallows.

In 1474, a rooster was put on trial in a small town on the Istrian Peninsula, charged with having laid an egg. The defense attorney was no match for the well-prepared prosecution. The gender-defying cock was found guilty and, reportedly, was burned at the stake with all the solemnity of a regular execution.

An elephant named Topsy was executed at the Coney Island amusement park in 1903. She had killed two handlers in Texas before being brought to New York, where she spent her days in chains, giving rides to noisy visitors and carrying heavy loads used in the construction of various park attractions. One evening, a drunken handler taunted the tired elephant and tried to feed her a lighted cigarette. Topsy had evidently had enough. She lifted the man with her trunk and threw him to the ground. He died instantly. The elephant was condemned to death by her owners—showmen who smelled opportunity. By advertising, they attracted a crowed of over 1,000 to watch as Topsy was fed cyanide-laced carrots. Nothing happened. The owners called in Thomas Edison. A proponent of direct current, Edison had an ulterior motive; he wanted to show that Westinghouse's alternating current was so dangerous, it could kill an elephant. He was right. Fifteen hundred people showed up one cold Sunday in January to watch as three-ton Topsy was zapped with 6,600 volts of electricity for ten seconds. The elephant was duly executed.

You are expendable, unwanted, despised. We cast you out forever. This is the message given the condemned—be they human or beast. Even so, it can be a long road between the public ritual of condemnation and that last moment of finality, especially in high-tech, modern-day America.

Waiting: Life on the Edge of the Abyss

☹ Hangman. The game. Played solo, at night, on our lonely computers, or with pen and paper in hospital hallways, waiting with worried friends and family members.

The game of "Hangman" is an easy distraction. You start with the gallows—a simple construction of four parts: a straight line foundation, a tall vertical pole, the horizontal bar on top, and, hanging from that, a simple noose. Hangman is a word game. The player has only six chances to find the letters to make a designated word. With each miss, a part of the condemned man takes shape. First miss—draw the head in the noose. Second miss, draw a stick body. Third missed letter, draw an arm. The other arm and two stick legs follow.

You lose the game when your little stick man is fully assembled and hanging from the gallows tree. Draw a straight line for the mouth and two Xs for the dead man's eyes. The end.

Life on death row is something like the game of Hangman. The condemned die a little bit at a time. The actual execution, that last dramatic hour, is only the tag end of a long process of erasure.

It all begins with the crime and the bewilderment or haze of that moment of passion or rage or insanity or accident or the calculated clean-up after a premeditated act. In the aftermath there is the exposure or confession or the sense of being hunted, the hiding, the heartbeats, the confusion and the capture.

From the moment of capture, (whether you committed the crime or are falsely accused) life turns upside down. In a book about her 1964 imprisonment for civil rights protests in Albany, Georgia, pacifist activist Barbara Deming reminisced about her first arrest, in 1962, after protesting nuclear testing. She was sent to the Women's House of Detention. She was not on death row. Her imprisonment for participating in this protest would be only a short stint, a day or two. Still, in her prison memoir she recalled the experience common to all of the imprisoned, of being made "the other"—someone set apart from the rest of humanity.

> Nobody has to print in a manual for guards that the prisoner must be wished out of existence for society's sake; this magic principle is grasped as if by instinct. Prison routine varies from place to place, but the one blind effort shapes it everywhere. Here is part of the routine of our "admission" that day:
>
> A policewoman takes us into a small room in the building where we are arraigned. She searches our handbags for sharp objects; we take off most of our clothing for her, unfasten the rest as she peers at us. . . . I am led into a large shower room and told to strip. Another guard shakes out each piece of clothing. Hand on her hips, she watches me closely as I take my shower, and I struggle hard now for self-possession. Her stance reminds me a little of that of an animal trainer. Now she asks me to hold my arms wide for a moment, turn my back and squat. I ask the reason. She, too, is searching for dope—or for concealed weapons. . . . I am given a very short hospital gown and led now into a small medical-examination room. Another of my companions is just leaving the room and smiles at me wanly. I climb up on the table. I assume that the examination performed is to check for venereal disease. The woman in the white smock grins at me and then at her assistant, who grins back. No, this too is a search for concealed dope or dangerous weapons.
>
> I hear myself laugh weakly. Can they frisk us any further now? . . . They wouldn't be able to admit it to themselves, but their search, of course, is for something else, and is efficient: their search is for our pride. And I think with a sinking heart: again and again, it must be, they find it and take it.

A Lesson before Dying by Ernest J. Gaines, a novel written in 1993, is about racism and being made the "other." It is about one prisoner's struggle to find dignity before he is put to death. In the story, Jefferson, a young black man in a small Cajun community, is falsely accused of murder. During the trial, his condescending lawyer defends him, telling the twelve white jurors, "Gentlemen of the jury, be merciful. For God's sake, be merciful. He is innocent of all charges brought against him.

But let us say he was not. Let us for a moment say he was not. What justice would there be to take this life? Justice, gentlemen? Why, I would just as soon put a hog in the electric chair as this."

Jefferson is quickly found guilty and sentenced to death, but the death sentence is not what is tormenting the accused, or his loving godmother, Miss Emma. She is beside herself with humiliation, saying, "They called my boy a hog. . . . I didn't raise no hog, and I don't want no hog to go set in that chair. I want a man to go set in that chair." She knows it is too late to save Jefferson. All Miss Emma can hope for now is that he will somehow manage to die with dignity. To that end, she persuades university-educated Grant Wiggins to do something for his people and help Jefferson die with dignity. It won't be easy. Jefferson, alone in his death row cell, feels himself to be less than human. In the few months before his execution, Jefferson and the reluctant Wiggins forge a bond and teach each other about dignity and heroism. This is "the lesson before dying."

Cliff Frasier, a United Church of Christ minister, was arrested at a November, 2002, faith-based action to close down the infamous "School of the Americas" (renamed by the Bush administration "The Western Hemisphere Institute for Security Cooperation")—a combat-training school for Latin American soldiers and assassins, located in Columbus, Georgia. After his arrest, Reverend Frasier spent a night in the Muscogee county jail—a night that transformed the way he looks at the world. Like Barbara Deming and the fictional Jefferson, Reverend Frasier observed the process of dehumanization inherent in the prison setting. Later, in a 2003 sermon, as he prepared to become a "prisoner of conscience" and serve a six-month sentence, he described one insight from his memorable night:

> From my one night in the Muscogee jail, I learned that the prison environment is meant to remove all traces of God's creation and human creativity as well. As we were incarcerated, it was clear: gone were the small objects suggesting grace or hinting of right-relationship in the world. The flowers were gone, the pictures were gone, the little things that I take for granted. Gone were the small curlicues in the corners of the woodwork, which some craftsman thought of putting there just for others to see. As if a speck of beauty was a dangerous thing—as if it could communicate compassion, as if a curlicue could send a message or suggest: we are meant

to build a world which is nurturing for one another and in-balance. All of these were removed.

There was only one kind of beauty that remained: traces of dignity and beauty in the human form could not be purged. After the sky was gone and the curlicues were gone, what was left were suggestions of God's grace carved in us. Guards and the prisoners alike shared fingerprints of God's creation.

Although all prisoners experience the desolation and despair of handcuffs and cell bars, a capital trial holds special horror. Trials commonly involve long hallways, long waits, hurried lawyers recounting the same details over and over, the judge, the accusers, the jurors, the smell of the courthouse, the oversized furniture designed to dwarf humans. At the end of that process comes the verdict. For the person sentenced to death, it doesn't matter what happened before—if we were good or bad at the tasks of our lives (parenting, holding a job, expressing ourselves with words, art, or music). None of that matters now. At sentencing we hear the proclamation that all of society wishes us dead for the thing we've done, for the one thing everyone knows about that we've done.

Part of the reality of capital punishment is its power to make the condemned disappear from view. Between the exposure and public condemnation of the courtroom and the day of execution, stretch years in a world rendered almost invisible to the rest of society.

In the famous stories by J. K. Rowling, Harry Potter and his non-"Muggle" friends must catch a scarlet steam engine, the Hogwarts Express, to get to school. The train leaves from London's King's Cross station, platform nine and three-quarters. The thing is, between platforms nine and ten is nothing but a dividing barrier. Hogwarts students run at the barrier and disappear from sight, entering a world that is invisible to the rest of London.

Death row inmates are a little like Hogwarts students, except that, instead of catching a magical scarlet steam engine to great adventures, they catch the train straight to an invisible hell, neatly and utterly removed from the rest of society.

❖ *Where there is invisibility there is often ignorance. . . . There is a common misperception, for example, that death row inmates have unlimited access to cable television and modern exercise equipment. In Texas, inmates spend twenty-three hours a day in a sixty-square-foot cell that*

*has four solid walls and a slit of a window. None can have a television. . . .
There is no air conditioning, despite summer temperatures that routinely
approach one-hundred degrees. Conditions are similar in Oklahoma, except that the entire death row facility is underground, so there is no natural light. In Oklahoma, a death sentence means never seeing sunshine again.*

~ DAVID R. DOW

It is not the person, alone in the world, at the moment of his or her
execution that makes the death penalty barbaric—though the moment
of execution *is* barbaric. It is not that moment of being strapped to the
gurney and injected with poison, or the moment when the hood is
drawn over the head or the noose put around the neck, or the moment
when the switch is thrown—though these moments *are* barbaric.

It is, more than anything else, the torment of the time—months?
years?—leading up to the execution that is the heart of the outrage.
People on death row must hear themselves condemned to death, must
know themselves to be cast out of human society, the ultimate exclu-
sion. Then, they must wait for death, virtually buried alive in small
cages, deprived of almost everything the rest of us take for granted—
the ability to make small decisions about when and what to eat, when
to turn off the light and go to bed, the option to be called by name,
the assumption of mobility (in this most mobile of all societies), the
pleasure of human contact, the expectation of being cared for if we get
sick. This is the stuff of daily life, forbidden or sharply restricted on
death row.

❖ *The mind-numbing, soul-killing savage sameness that makes each day
an echo of the day before, with neither thought nor hope of growth, makes
prison the abode of spirit death that it is for over a million men and
women now held in U.S. hellholes.*

~ MUMIA ABU-JAMAL

❖ *A condemned prisoner can survey his whole house with one quick sweep
of his eyes: It is essentially a bathroom with a bunk where the tub would
ordinarily be. He spends an average of twenty-three hours a day inside,
knows every hairline crack and rusty paint chip. If this is a winter morning, it is very cold on death row; if this is summer, it is very hot. It stinks
the same regardless of the season, the air thick with the odor of smoking,
sweating, dirty, defecating men.*

~ DAVID VON DREHLE

MEDITATION ON FEELING CONFINED

Think back to your least favorite class in middle school or high school. Perhaps it was the subject you hated most or didn't understand, (math? chemistry? Latin?) or a subject you understood so well you were bored out of your mind.

Perhaps the classroom itself was the enemy, with its thickly painted cream-colored walls and lack of visuals, nothing to look at as you sat on your hard little chair. Remember how you hated those walls and those chairs?

Remember watching the hands of the clock? Were they stuck? Had time stopped? Remember the monotony of the mediocre teacher or the scowling, bitter teacher with the mean streak? Remember how it felt to know that you would have to return the next day and the next?

You couldn't wait to get out of that room, to get a breath of air or pass a quick note to a friend or grab a drink at the water fountain or just move your body or do anything but sit there for another minute. Remember feeling that you just had to get out of there?

Now shrink that memory of the four, barren classroom walls and the boredom, into the shape of an even smaller room. Imagine endless days of sameness, of sameness and sameness, of loud noises, bright lights, the total absence of any decision-making about food or sleep or activity.

Some of the people who supervise you will have a heart and an ability to reason, and some will not. Some will be worse than your worst memory of the boring teacher or the bitter one with the mean streak.

You will stay here, entombed, in a demented dream of detention, for twenty-three hours a day, every day of every week, and every week of every month, and every month of every year for a very long stretch of mind-numbing, soul-numbing years until you are put to death. Your execution date shifts now and then, as court appeals come and go. The day of your pre-scheduled death and the way you'll die loom large on the barren landscape.

Finally, death row is about the sounds of the man a few cells away who has completely lost his mind and howls day and night, and it is about no hope, no hope at all. The people on death row must know ahead of time, not only how they will die, but the actual times and dates of their deaths.

❖ *A person is placed on death row and told that he or she will be killed. The authorities plan it, there is a ceremony and procedure, and the damned sits there, year after year, continually reminded that "We are going to kill you—but not yet. This is how we are going to kill you—but not yet. We are going to electrocute you, or gas you, or give you a lethal injection—but not yet." It is the ultimate torture and barbaric treatment of a fellow human being.*

~ROBERT R. BRYAN

Which Postures Fit the Penalty?
Methods of Execution—
From the Cross to the Syringe

📖 Short Story, "In the Penal Colony" by Franz Kafka (1919)

An explorer arrives at a penal colony where an officer shows him a unique and elegant execution machine called the Harrow. The condemned person lies face-down on a bed while a complex system of needles passes back and forth over him, piercing his flesh. The accused is essentially tattooed to death with the commandment, HONOR THY SUPERIORS.

As the officer prepares to execute a man accused of sleeping on duty, he explains to the uneasy visitor that the faces of those put to death on the Harrow are often gloriously transfigured by the torment.

Before the story ends, it is the officer himself lying face down under the needles. As the Harrow inscribes BE JUST, *it begins to malfunction and go to pieces.*

If a method of torture and execution can be imagined, it has been used. Count on it.

There is the crouching death, met on one's knees: as in a beheading at the guillotine or a stoning. In the 13th century, in the Iraqi city of

A slow day at the guillotine

Mosul, an early Yazidi saint was executed as a crowd pelted him with heads of lettuce.

There is death met upright: crucified, burned at the stake, impaled on a sharp object that splits the body up the middle, or strangled on a garrote, an iron collar, or stood up against a wall, with or without a blindfold, to be gunned down by firing squad.

There is death met while still moving—walking the gauntlet, or stuffed into a bag and thrown from a cliff, or hanged on a gallows tree (also known as "swinging," "dancing on nothing" or "kicking the air") with a noose around one's neck.

Sometimes, one method of execution is just not enough. In 1606 Guy Fawkes, the infamous explosives expert hired by conspirators to blow up England's House of Lords, was multiply executed. First, he was hanged, then he was disemboweled, beheaded, and quartered at Old Palace Yard, Westminster.

There is death met seated: in a chair, head back—suffocated by a combination of water and cloth, or by molten lead poured into one's mouth, or, in our modern age, strapped into an electric chair or in a gas chamber, waiting for cyanide pellets to poison the air.

If it can be imagined, it has been done.

> *Dont-Care didn't care;*
> *Dont-care was wild.*
> *Dont-care stole plum and pear*
> *Like any beggar's child.*
> *Dont-care was made to care,*
> *Dont-care was hung:*
> *Dont-care was put in the pot*
> *And boiled till he was done.*
>
> ~ANONYMOUS

There is death met lying down: dismembered on a rack, stretched until torn apart, or crushed by heavy weights such as boulders or elephants, or strapped to a gurney in a sterile room while lethal chemicals are injected through a syringe—one, two, three.

In the current American mythology, lethal injection (invented and first used in 1939 against "defective children" by Dr. Karl Brandt, the personal physician of Adolf Hitler) is preferred because it is assumed to be "humane," virtually pain-free, apart from the insertion of the needle into the vein. Sister Helen Prejean, author of the book *Dead Man Walking*, disputes this, urging us to think beyond the concern with physical discomfort to the truth of lethal injection:

> There remains, however, one dimension of suffering that can never be eliminated when death is imposed on a conscious human being: the horror of being put to death against your will and the agony of anticipation. As if, when they strap you down on the gurney, your arms outstretched, waiting for the silent deadly fluid to flow—the sodium pentothol, which comes first to make you unconscious so you do not feel the pancuronium bromide when it paralyzes your diaphragm and stops your breathing and the potassium chloride which causes cardiac arrest and stops your heart—as if you feel the terror of death any less because chemicals are being used to kill you instead of electricity or bullets or rope?
>
> There is an elaborate ruse going on here, a pitiful disguise. Killing is camouflaged as a medicinal act. The attendant will even swab

the "patient's" arm with alcohol before inserting the needle—to prevent infection.

Kenneth Stewart, one of the condemned who was allowed to make a choice, chose the electric chair over lethal injection for his September 23, 1998, execution by the state of Virginia. In explanation, he said,

> Two thousand years ago, they put my Lord and Savior to death on a cross. This gurney back here is the exact same thing. It's just a cross laid down, your arms outstretched. They don't have the nails no more, but they have the steel needles that pierce your skin.

Posture has not been incidental to the execution process throughout history. It only ceased to matter when executions disappeared from public participation.

❖ *The move to lethal injection continued the long-term trend away from visual display at executions. A public hanging had involved grand gestures by a condemned person standing on a stage, before crowds numbering in the thousands. A hanging in the jail yard was a similar ceremony before a smaller audience. In an electric chair or a gas chamber the condemned prisoner was seated, not standing, and the audience was still smaller. Now, with lethal injection, the condemned person was lying down. The sense that death lying down was undignified had played a part in the design of the electric chair and gas chamber, but that sense had nearly vanished by the end of the century. Now few saw any significance in the posture of the condemned person.*

~STUART BANNER

In the United States today, executions have become mundane (albeit high-tech) bureaucratic affairs to which the public is not invited. Many opponents of the death penalty believe executions carried out as if in secret are proving a dangerous trend. In 1994, Phil Donahue proposed televising an execution on his talk show. The condemned man agreed, but a federal court denied the request.

Another opponent of capital punishment, Senator Mark Hatfield, unsuccessfully introduced a bill requiring TV coverage of the rare federal execution.

Timothy McVeigh wanted his government-sponsored death televised, as did many citizens who jumped into the debate in the spring of

2001. Some would-be viewers, like Mike Wallace of *60 Minutes*, argued that such coverage would act as a deterrent to crime by showing the sorry consequences of violent action. Others simply wanted the opportunity to see McVeigh "get what was coming to him." In the end, however, a *Time*/CNN poll found that 80 percent of Americans were opposed to televising the execution.

Death row and the execution chamber, like the rest of what Pulitzer Prize–winning journalist Joseph T. Hallinan calls our "prison nation" (*Going up the River: Travels in a Prison Nation*), are hidden from view, out of sight, out of mind, out of conscience. When I began writing this book, a friend asked, in a most bewildered voice, "Why on earth would you write a book about the death penalty? What has it got to do with you?" To him, clearly, this seemed a remote topic, an academic question, a distasteful subject that was utterly beside the point of our sophisticated lives. We are not disturbed by what we never see.

Sister Helen Prejean, like many abolitionists, is in favor of making executions public again. In *Dead Man Walking*, she wrote about being interviewed by ABC's Peter Jennings opposite political commentator George Will. Will was against televising executions on the basis that it would have a coarsening effect on the public, to which Prejean responded in her book,

> But it's not the presence of television cameras or the composition of the crowd or even whether the crowd acts politely or not that makes the execution of a human being ugly. An execution is ugly because the premeditated killing of a human being is ugly. Torture is ugly. Gassing, hanging, shooting, electrocuting, or lethally injecting a person whose hands and feet are tied is ugly. And hiding the ugliness from view and rationalizing it numbs our minds to the horror of what we are doing. This is what truly "coarsens" us.

Other death penalty opponents disagree. In *Legal Lynching*, co-written by Reverend Jesse Jackson, his legislator-son, Jesse, Jr., and Yale University professor Bruce Shapiro, the authors doubt that televising executions would shame or shock viewers into opposing capital punishment. They quote author-psychologist David Grossman, who says that America has developed a "new cult of vengeance." With Grossman, they argue:

Television and movie audiences easily learn to associate images of inflicted death with "entertainment, pleasure, their favorite soft drink, their favorite candy bar and the close, intimate contact of their date." And what they remember, even when the bad guys get their just desserts, is not the law but the vengeance.

This is America in the age of "reality TV." Just when we think TV programming can't get any cruder, along comes a new "Fear Factor" or "Survivor." Is it far-fetched to wonder if televised executions might be packaged as "Execution Night Last Minute Make-overs" or "Death Row Bachelor's Final Rejection"? Any night of the week, we can watch live action "Cops" and see real people being arrested in their underwear or witness high-speed car crashes at busy intersections. We've seen birth, we've seen death, we channel surf until something else catches our eye.

❖ *The ministers of Sainte Guillotine are robed and ready. Crash!—a head is held up, and the knitting-women, who scarcely lifted their eyes to look at it a moment ago when it could think and speak, count One.*

The second tumbril empties and moves on; the third comes up. Crash!—And the knitting-women, never faltering or pausing in their work, count Two.

~FROM *A TALE OF TWO CITIES* BY CHARLES DICKENS

2

Three Myths about the Death Penalty

📖 Two Short Stories: "The Ones Who Walk Away from Omelas" by Ursula K. Le Guin, in *The Wind's Twelve Quarters*, and "The Lottery" by Shirley Jackson.

Omelas is the name of Le Guin's "bright-towered" imaginary city by the sea, a seemingly idyllic place that inspires "a boundless and generous contentment" in its citizens. Every year it plays host to the Festival of Summer, and people come from far and wide to see the processions and to celebrate.

Far below the city, in a dark, dank, airless broom closet, with its foul-smelling mops, a child is locked away. The child—naked, neglected, and covered with sores—is afraid of the mops. If someone comes with a half-bowl of corn meal and grease, the child may cry, "Please let me out. I will be good!" No one is listening. No one cares. No one hears.

Everyone in shining, happy Omelas knows about the child. Sometimes they descend to the closet to stare and to listen to the miserable creature cry. Most often they feel resentment and disgust at what they see, but not pity. They believe that, if the child were brought up into the sunlight, cleaned and fed, "in that day and hour all the prosperity and beauty and delight of Omelas would wither and be destroyed." These are the terms, or so the citizens believe.

In Shirley Jackson's more famous story "The Lottery," the good people of a certain small town believe that their happiness depends on the annual ritual of selecting one of their friendly neighbors to be stoned to death.

At the end of Jackson's story, the characters quietly return to their comfortable homes, but Le Guin suggests that, what Hannah Arendt called the "banality of evil" is not inevitable. Her story title honors the occasional few who,

having seen the miserable child in the closet, do not return home, but walk out
of the city, straight through the beautiful gates of Omelas, into unknown dark-
ness, as if they know where they are going.

The Myth of Closure

Those of us who oppose the death penalty are often taunted with the accusation, "You'd be for the death penalty too, if someone you loved was murdered." This statement is rooted in both an assumed desire for revenge and in the myth of "closure"—something family members of the victim are supposed to find after an execution.

The word "closure" implies a shift in point of view or perspective, from *before* to *after*. The before is the unfinished business of waiting for the scales of justice to be balanced with a life for a life. The after is the anticipated sense of completion or relief the victim's loved ones are supposed to feel when the accused murderer is dead.

For Antoinette Bosco it was not that simple. Her heart broke when a teenager shot and killed both her son and daughter-in-law, but, after a long period of grief and confusion, she found healing in forgiving the murderer. In her book, *Choosing Mercy*, she explained:

> It had become almost routine to say that only if a murderer is put to death could a victim's family find "closure." I detested that word, because I saw it as meaningless. What was it—a door slammed shut, the end of breathing, a body-filled box put into the ground, a heart permanently hardened? . . . choosing such "closure" would keep all of us in a closed, fixed place, perpetually unhealed. . . . I was already getting used to being questioned about my position, with people saying they couldn't understand how I could forgive the murderer of my son and daughter-in-law. Some would actually accuse me of not loving my children if I didn't want the murderer to get the same fate that he had dished out. My answer was that, on the contrary, I was honoring my murdered children by raising my voice against killing, all killing.

Sandra Miller was another mother who learned that witnessing an execution does not automatically bring closure. Her son was kidnapped from a bus stop and became one of the fourteen victims murdered by the "Freeway Killer," William George Bonin. More than a decade later—a long stretch of painful years during which she became an alcoholic, had two heart attacks and attempted suicide several times—Miller was in the crowd of witnesses at Bonin's execution where she hoped to "finalize this pain." Two years after the execution, however, she came to the realization that there would be no finality. "It doesn't bring closure. I hate that word. They should've never invented it. It's an impossible thing. Nothing can bring closure to the death of a child."

Another grieving mother, Aba Gayle, believes that the idea of closure is perpetuated by prosecutors. She calls it "the big lie—we will catch him, we will convict him, we will execute him, and you'll be OK." Gayle held onto this like a lifeline when her nineteen-year-old daughter was murdered, but after years of anger and rage, she chose another path to healing. She began to study meditation and read books about Christianity, Buddhism, and Hinduism. When she eventually wrote a letter to her daughter's murderer, he wrote back. She expressed forgiveness, he remorse. She started visiting him on death row at least twice a year, and her healing began.

❖ *Misery justice is our dominant system. It purports to create justice by making everyone equally miserable. It does nothing to help the victims, but creates a level playing field by re-victimizing them while making offenders equally miserable.*

~RUTH MORRIS

It is a myth that everyone mourning the murder of a loved one finds closure at an execution, as if the horror of memory and the grief of loss somehow magically vanish or diminish at five minutes past the murderer's date with death.

Stories of Healing

For some, healing comes from breaking the cycle of violence. We need to hear their stories.

Every now and then a crime makes national headlines, grabs top billing on television newscasts, rivets our attention, and is so universally abhorrent, that we are united in outrage. Such was the case in 1998, when three white men in Texas attacked James Byrd, Jr., a black man. They beat him, spray-painted his face, pulled down his pants, chained him by the ankles to the bumper of a pickup truck, and dragged him up and down back country roads. In the process, he was slowly skinned alive, dismembered, and, ultimately, decapitated.

Who didn't feel like screaming for the death penalty then?

As it turns out, Byrd's own son didn't—not after he had some time to think about it. On the Fourth of July, 2002, Ross Byrd led a 24-hour prayer vigil and fast on behalf of John W. "Bill" King, one of the men sentenced to death for this crime. The convicted man's appeals were almost used up and an execution date was imminent. Other people fasted and prayed with Byrd, including Martin Luther King, III, son of the slain civil rights leader.

Byrd mentioned three reasons for his change of heart. First, he realized that executing his father's killers would not ease his pain. Second, he said that, "To want to see the men who killed my daddy die by the state, is the same for me to go out and kill them myself." Third, he was guided by a religious teaching, saying, "It's the big picture we're trying to look at, and the big picture is God says, THOU SHALL NOT KILL."

Evidently, big hearts run in the Byrd family. The members of this anguished family have worked through their grief and rage by taking positive action and founding the James Byrd Jr. Foundation For Racial Healing.

Another crime that made national headlines was the murder (some say "crucifixion") of Matthew Shepard in Laramie, Wyoming. He was a slight, gentle, soft-spoken, openly gay, 21-year-old college freshman. One cold October night in 1998, he was lured from a bar by two young men and driven to a remote area outside of Laramie. There, he was savagely pistol-whipped with the butt of a handgun, repeatedly kicked in the groin, tied to a fence, beaten some more, robbed of his shoes and his wallet, which contained $20, and was left, moaning on the fence, to die alone. Part of the horror was that he did not die that night. He was discovered, still alive, eighteen hours later, by a bicyclist who, seeing the crumpled body propped upright on the lonely prairie, thought at first he had found a strange scarecrow. Later, the sheriff's deputy would testify that Shepard's head was almost entirely covered in blood, except for a clean spot "where he'd been crying and the tears went down his face." Shepard died after four days in the hospital.

Who didn't feel like screaming for the death penalty then?

As it turns out, Shepard's own parents didn't. They helped negotiate life sentences for the two killers. At a sentencing hearing, Dennis

Shepard spoke in the hushed courtroom, directly addressing one of his son's murderers, saying, "I give you life in the memory of one who no longer lives."

Judy Shepard's grief at her son's murder transformed her. She began by studying issues central to the gay community, then researched several gay rights activist groups and, when she was ready, this reserved Wyoming housewife found her voice. She used her place in the media spotlight to advocate for hate crimes legislation and for the goal of building a society that celebrates diversity and encourages tolerance. She has been quoted as saying, "Matthew would be very disappointed in me if I gave up."

People who argue against the death penalty are routinely accused of not caring about the victims of crime. The assumption seems to be that we must choose "sides"; we are either on the "side" of the murder victim and the victim's family or we are on the "side" of the person found guilty of committing the murder. Now, when those of us who oppose the death penalty are taunted with the accusation, "You'd be for the death penalty too, if someone you loved was murdered," we can tell the story of Matthew Shepard's parents, as well as of the families of James Byrd and Martin Luther King, Jr.

We could add to that list the man who, through several decades of the late twentieth century, was considered America's number-one TV Dad, Bill Cosby. On January 16, 1997, his only son, Ennis, a 27-year-old Columbia University student, was shot to death while changing a tire on a Bel Air roadside. Mikhail Markhasev, a Ukrainian immigrant, was arrested for the crime and later convicted of first-degree murder and attempted robbery. According to news stories, the Cosby family requested that prosecutors not seek the death penalty, and Markhasev was sentenced to life without parole.

Norman Felton (the Hollywood writer, director, and producer best known for "The Man from U.N.C.L.E." and "Dr. Kildare") and his wife Aline are two more to add to the list. Around midnight, on December 22, 1982, they got terrible news. Their youngest daughter, Betsy, a law student in Detroit, and Betsy's husband David, had been found stabbed to death. Their baby, Jessica, had been stabbed to death as well.

Eventually, three men were brought to trial for the murders. They had been on drugs, desperate for money to buy more drugs, crazed with violence. It was testified in court that Betsy had been raped, then was made to watch as her baby was stabbed to death, before she too was killed.

Who didn't feel like screaming for the death penalty then?

The Feltons, Betsy's parents, didn't. The media were quick to pounce on this gruesome, Christmastime triple murder. But when Norman Felton heard people demanding the death penalty, he felt called to speak out. He said, "Our family has never believed in the death penalty and I can't say at this moment, although I'm torn by what has happened to my daughter, David, and baby Jessica, that I can change the way I feel. Because if what I feel has any meaning, then am I going to change my beliefs because somebody in my family is murdered? It would make it a ridiculous farce."

The judge echoed the public's cry for death. At the time, however, Michigan didn't have the death penalty, and so the three men were convicted and sentenced to life without possibility of parole.

The Feltons attended several meetings of Parents of Murdered Children, where the abolition of capital punishment is not a popular point of view. They spoke up anyway, urging positive action as the best route to healing. Furthermore, they took their own advice. They founded the "Jessica Fund" to support a day-care center in Detroit, the one Jessica would have attended if she'd lived to be a toddler.

Tariq Khamisa was a twenty-year-old student at San Diego State University, working part time delivering pizzas, when he was shot and killed by a fourteen-year-old gang member, in 1995. Tariq's father, Azim Khamisa, was devastated and, for months, could barely get out of bed in the morning. A devout Muslim, he sought spiritual counseling and was encouraged to do good deeds to help speed the journey of his son's soul. He subsequently founded the Tariq Khamisa Foundation (TKF), an organization dedicated to stopping children from killing children.

The grieving father went a step further. Taking inspiration from the life of Mohandas Gandhi who said, "We must become the change we wish to see in the world," he reached out to the family of the young murderer. Azim Khamisa explained, "It has been my view from the beginning that there were victims on both sides of the gun." By reaching out he found Ples Felix, a grandfather devastated by a grandson's crime of violence.

The alliance of the victim's anguished father and the assailant's grieving grandfather has gained national attention as the two men tour the country, talking to schoolchildren about guns, gangs, violence, revenge, and forgiveness. "I will mourn Tariq's death for the rest of my life," says Azim Khamisa. "Now, however, my grief has been transformed into a powerful commitment to change."

Murder Victims Families for Reconciliation
There are many more stories to be told, of positive action taken in the wake of tragedy, action that satisfies and heals. One organization, Murder Victims Families for Reconciliation (MVFR), makes such stories its focal point. Founded in 1976, MVFR is a national organization of murder victims' families who oppose the death penalty. According to the group, "Reconciliation means accepting that you cannot undo the murder but you can decide how you want to live afterward."

MVFR was founded by Marie Deans whose mother-in-law was murdered. According to Deans, "The death penalty is a false God promising to bring justice and closure to victims' families. There is no justice for murder. You cannot give enough time in prison and you cannot kill enough people to make up for the precious, unique human life that murder takes. Instead, we must put the vast resources we spend on killing a small percentage of murderers into preventing homicides."

Robert Renny Cushing has served as the Executive Director of MVFR. Like the other board members, his involvement comes from direct experience of tragedy. One day in June, 1988, his father answered a knock at the front door and was blown apart by a shotgun blast. Later, a rogue cop, guilty of a host of bad actions, turned himself in.

After his father's bloody death, Cushing remained opposed to the death penalty. He said, "Healing is a process, not an event. I don't presume to prescribe a way to heal for other people, I just know for myself that healing does not come from murdering people." The guilty officer and the officer's wife, an accomplice in the murder, were both given sentences of life without parole.

Ten years after the murder, Cushing, serving then as a New Hampshire State Representative, introduced an amendment to eliminate the death penalty.

Bud Welch has also served on the board of MVFR. His daughter, Julie Marie, was killed in 1995, with 167 others, at the Murrah Federal

Building in Oklahoma City. Although he was initially overwhelmed with a desire for revenge, he later realized that the death penalty is "all about revenge and hate, and revenge and hate is why Julie and 167 others are dead today." Welch worked against the execution of Timothy McVeigh, the young man found guilty of the terrorist bombing and executed in June, 2001. In a meeting with Bill McVeigh, the bomber's bewildered father, Welch had compassion. "I was able to tell him that I truly understood the pain he was going through, and that he—as I—was a victim of what had happened in Oklahoma City."

❖ *As time does—and will—reveal, forgiveness is a creative, transforming, healing force that breaks the cycle of violence and lights the way to the great community of brotherhood and sisterhood that is our highest calling—the reign of God.*

~BROTHER BERNIE SPITZLEY

The Myth of Deterrence

❖ *It makes sense that the death penalty should stop people from killing. It also makes sense that a boulder should fall to the ground faster than a wad of paper. But in both cases, common sense is wrong. Some states with no death penalty have very low murder rates; others with vigorous death penalties have astronomical murder rates (Florida, for example). There are cases of sons who watched their fathers hang—a pretty stern deterrent message—who went on to commit capital offenses themselves. There are even cases of hangmen who were later hanged.*

~DAVID VON DREHLE

It is time to debunk the myth that capital punishment is an effective tool in the war against crime. Politicians and bureaucrats benefit from touting "deterrence." By simply endorsing the death penalty, they sound tough on crime. It is a meaningless boast.

There is no evidence that the death penalty has ever functioned as a deterrent to crime. Until 1808, England imposed the death penalty for pickpocketing. Even so, pickpockets prided themselves on "working" the execution crowds. This sounds like a bad joke, except that it is true. And still, we have not learned.

❖ *We have been killing people for millions of years in the name of law, order, and God, and it hasn't put a dent in the crime or homicide rate. It has increased.*

~ROBERT R. BRYAN

Studies are almost unanimous in concluding that the death penalty is not a deterrent to crime; common sense tells us the same thing. If capital punishment acted as a deterrent, why would Texas, California, and Florida, three states with flourishing death rows, continue to have hundreds of murders each year?

❖ *If capital punishment were indeed the decisive deterrent to social mayhem that its proponents maintain, then Texas . . . would be nirvana with freeways.*

~STEVEN G. KELLMAN

Jasper is a town located in the heart of "Deep East Texas." As discussed earlier in this chapter, it made headline news in 1998 as the site of a horrendous crime: three white men tied a black man to the back of their truck and dragged the man to his death. Jasper is just up the road from Huntsville, the "ground zero" of capital punishment. Although Huntsville boasts a university, dozens of churches, several golf courses, parks, and lakes, and the Sam Houston Memorial Museum, it is known for its seven prisons as well as the busiest death chamber in the nation.

By all accounts, the frequent executions have become fairly ho-hum in Huntsville. Lights in town used to dim and flicker when the electric chair was used, but lethal injection is as quiet as cancer. Huntsville's identity as the "prison-city" of the state is hardly concealed. It takes pride in its Texas Prison Museum, with execution paraphernalia on display, including the retired electric chair fondly known as "Old Sparky." A local diner serves a "Killer Burger" on execution days. And then there's the "Captain Joe Byrd Cemetery," located between a mobile-home park and a car wash. No one wants to be buried there. It is for those prisoners too poor to die, those with not a soul to claim the body. In the older section of the vast graveyard are headstones bearing the names of the deceased, but in the newer sections, most of the dead get only a cross with a date of death and a prison ID number.

Huntsville is like a great big neon sign on the death penalty landscape. It is garish and visible, hard to miss. Everyone in Texas knows something about Huntsville and its death chamber. People outside of Texas know about the Huntsville death chamber. It is hard to think about Huntsville without thinking about the death penalty. Even so, three men who lived just up the road from the nation's busiest death house were not deterred from committing their gruesome murder. Nor did it deter Andrea Yates, who methodically drowned her five children in the bathtub of her home in Houston, located just seventy miles south of Huntsville.

If people who live in the shadow of the nation's busiest death chamber are not deterred by the death penalty, who is?

❖ *At times, the deterrence myth bleeds over into outright lies or fantasy. In that October 2000 presidential debate, George W. Bush declared his capital-punishment apparatus in Texas part of a successful crime-fighting machine: "I'm proud of the fact that violent crime is down in the state of Texas. I'm proud of the fact that we hold people accountable."*

Bush's crime-fighting success, unfortunately, is a figment of his imagination. According to figures in the FBI's Uniform Crime Reports released in the same month as the Bush-Gore debate, while crime is declining in cities nationwide, it is rising in the large cities of Texas. . . . Why, then, does the deterrence myth persist? Police know the death penalty doesn't deter crime. Crime-policy experts know it. The scholars know it. It is only politicians, it seems, who have not heard the news.

~REVEREND JESSE L. JACKSON, SR., REPRESENTATIVE
JESSE L. JACKSON, JR., AND BRUCE SHAPIRO

The crumbling, vast, and antiquated San Quentin State Prison was built in 1852 to stem California's rampant lawlessness. It originally confined 455 men. Today, although the threat of incarceration obviously failed to stem lawlessness, the ever-expanding prison, dubbed the "money pit" for good reason, is bursting at its seams with approximately 6,000 inmates, over 600 of them on death row.

The death penalty looms large in the awareness and the wallets of Californians. Even so, the state's homicide rate increased nearly eleven percent in 2002, and murders continue to make headlines.

On the evening of February 1, 2002, seven-year-old Danielle van Dam curled up under blankets in her pink and purple second-story bedroom in an upscale San Diego suburb. She was abducted in the middle of the night. Her tiny, nude, decomposing body was found nearly a month later. California's death penalty had not deterred the man who killed her.

❖ *The problem with deterrence, as applied to aggravated murder, is that it assumes killers calculate risk and reward. The reality, with few exceptions, is that murderers are not clear-thinking people.*

~DAVID VON DREHLE

Florida ranks third, behind California and Texas, in the number of people it keeps locked in death row cells. The Sunshine State's elected bureaucrats have been using capital punishment like a cheap flag, waving it whenever they want to posture as tough on crime. Even so, the state is hardly an advertisement for the efficacy of capital punishment. Instead, it has a reputation for gang-violence and car-jackings.

A report on "Homicide Trends in the U.S." by the Bureau of Justice Statistics baldly states, "Rates of murder, and especially those involving guns, are higher in southern regions of the United States." The southern regions are also where the death penalty is more fervently endorsed. Further, statisticians have sometimes observed that murder rates increase directly following highly publicized executions. This was true in California, after the 1992 execution of Robert Harris, that state's first execution in twenty-five years. In the months following this execution, the number of homicides actually increased. The same thing happened after Oklahoma resumed executions and in Illinois after John Gacy was put to death.

Some theorize that, far from being a deterrent, the death penalty reinforces a climate of violence and acts to brutalize the population it would seek to protect.

❖ *On a school trip, Adam Pinkton went to the Mississippi State Penitentiary to see the gas chamber. Three years later, high on drugs, Adam shot Louis Coats. Adam could not spell* deterrence, *let alone contemplate its consequences. He was sentenced to death.*

~CLIVE STAFFORD-SMITH

The Myth of Proportionality
(or—Only the Worst-of-the-Worst
Get the Ultimate Punishment)

❖ *There seems to be a growing awareness that the death penalty is just another government program that doesn't work very well.*

~STEPHEN BRIGHT

By all accounts, John Spenkelink was doing OK in life until the age of eleven. He even had a paper route. All that changed the day he came home from school and found his father, dead, in the closed garage with the car running. After that, Spenkelink's life slipped out of control.

Who knows why, but he started down the path from troubled boy to bad boy (up to no good—sniffing glue, picking fights, stealing), from bad boy to scoundrel, and from scoundrel to outlaw, in and out of prison for holding up gas stations and grocery stores with the help of a .357 magnum.

Then one day in 1973, he picked up a hitchhiker who was considerably more depraved than he was. Joe Szymankiewicz had been in prison almost twenty years continuously, and was known for his vicious temperament.

In a Tallahassee motel room, Joe terrorized Spenkelink, making him play Russian roulette, forcing sex at gunpoint, and finally robbing him of all his money. At some point, Spenkelink left and picked up another hitchhiker, Frank Brumm. The two returned to the motel and killed Joe. Brumm hit him on the head with a hatchet, and Spenkelink used a gun.

Both men were charged with the killing, but they got two different lawyers, two different trial strategies, and two different results. Brumm was acquitted. Spenkelink, who had rejected the opportunity to plea bargain to a lesser charge, was convicted of first-degree murder and sentenced to death—which is what Spenkelink finally got: death.

On Friday, May 25, 1979, John Spenkelink, whose final months on death row had earned him the respect of guards and inmates alike, was strapped into Florida's electric chair. The witnesses, twelve observers and twelve reporters, sat in white wooden chairs with heart-shaped backs. When the blinds snapped open to expose the death chamber, the witnesses saw Spenkelink already seated in the electric chair. The chin strap was pulled so tightly, he physically couldn't speak his final words. After the signal was given, the hooded executioner had to throw the switch three times before the doctor pronounced Spenkelink dead. By then, the smoke of burning flesh was curling up from John's leg.

Two men murdered another. One was acquitted and walked free. The other was executed.

❖ *If you tried to sell death penalty stock on Wall Street, the Securities and Exchange Commission would have you prosecuted for fraud. Capital punishment doesn't achieve any of the things its backers promise it will, and it is a spectacular waste of time and money.*

~ROBERT SHERRILL

The randomness of our justice system pervades every prison hallway, cell by cell. On the one hand, there are the unlucky ones, whose severe sentences defy all logic. On March 16, 2000, a teenager in Tyler, Texas, was sentenced to sixteen years in prison for stealing a Snickers candy bar from a convenience store. The United States Supreme Court weighed in on a similar case, in March, 2003, upholding the fifty-year sentence of a man who was arrested for stealing a few videotapes for his nieces.

Contrast those long sentences with the mere seven years given Dan White, an ex-policeman. In 1978, he assassinated San Francisco Mayor Moscone and then walked down the hall and shot Harvey Milk, the first openly gay elected official in the United States. His famous excuse, later dubbed the "Twinkie Defense," was that he had become temporarily insane after eating too much junk food.

Sixteen years for stealing a candy bar. Fifty years for the theft of a few videotapes. Seven years—total—for the assassination of two people. There is not even a pretense of consistency in our fractured, fragmented, chaotic system.

❖ *Persons are sentenced to death and executed not because they have been found to be uncontrollably violent, hopelessly poor parole and release risks. Instead, they are executed for entirely different reasons. They have a poor defense at trial; they have no funds to bring sympathetic witnesses to court; they are immigrants or strangers in a community where they were tried; the prosecuting attorney wants the publicity that goes with sending a killer to the chair; they have inexperienced or overworked counsel at trial; there are no funds for an appeal or for a transcript of the trial record; they are members of a despised racial minority. In short, the actual study of why particular persons have been sentenced to death and executed does not show any careful winnowing of the worst from the bad.*

It shows instead that the executed were usually the unlucky victims of prejudice and discrimination, the losers in an arbitrary lottery that could just as well have spared them as killed them.

~HUGO BEDAU

Notorious Killers Who Were Not Sentenced to Death
Nationwide, only a small number of people found guilty of murder are sentenced to death row. The vast majority who have killed serve their sentences—long or short—in the general prison population.

Nor are the people on death row necessarily the worst-of-the-worst. Here is a list of some infamous killers who were spared the "ultimate punishment."

- James Earl Ray, accused assassin of Dr. Martin Luther King, Jr.
- Byron De La Beckwith, assassin of Mississippi civil rights leader Medgar Evers
- Mark David Chapman, killer of John Lennon (sentence: twenty to life)
- Charles Manson and the members of his California cult family
- David Berkowitz, a.k.a. "Son of Sam" (sentence: 365 to life)
- Jeffrey Dahmer, Wisconsin's neat and tidy cannibal (sentenced to close to one thousand years, he was killed by another prisoner two years into his sentence)
- Joel Rifkin, murderer of seventeen women (sentence: 203 to life)
- the Beverly Hills golden boys, Lyle and Erik Menendez. They killed their wealthy parents, then went on a shopping spree for new cars and Rolex watches. (sentence: life)
- Susan Smith, a white woman in South Carolina who murdered her toddler sons, then made up a story about a black carjacker (sentence: thirty to life)
- Robert Chambers, the "preppie killer." While awaiting trial, he mugged for a video camera, twisting off a doll's head and joking, "Oops, I think I killed it." He served fifteen years of his five-to-fifteen year sentence and is now free.
- Thomas Koskovich and Jayson Vreeland, teenagers who lured two pizza deliverymen to an abandoned house in rural New Jersey with a fake pizza order, then killed them, "simply for the experience." Both are serving life sentences.

Why was John Spenkelink executed while these were not? According to Robert Jay Lifton and Greg Mitchell, authors of *Who Owns Death?*, the United States death penalty protocol is nearly as arbitrary today as it was in 1972, when the Supreme Court temporarily halted it in *Furman v. Georgia*. According to Lifton and Mitchell,

> . . . it could hardly be otherwise, in a country with fifty states, each with its own laws covering executions. Even within the same state,

procedures for prosecuting capital cases vary from county to county. And this doesn't even begin to take into account the luck of the lottery—the fact that a prisoner's fate is often determined mainly by the makeup of a jury and the competence of his attorney, not the brutality of his crime.

Inconsistences in Illinois bothered then-Governor George Ryan. In his famous speech, following the January, 2003, decision to commute the sentences of all prisoners on his state's death row, he said:

> Now here's a good number for you to remember: In Illinois last year we had about 1,000 murders, and only 2 percent of that 1,000 were sentenced to death. I want to know, where is the fairness and equality in that?

The ones who do get sentenced to death can only marvel at the majority of murderers whose lives are spared. We can wonder with them—are they to die while the Son of Sam (Berkowitz) and the Menendez brothers live? Why? We can also ask—do the men and women on death row deserve the same punishment given to unrepentant mass-murderer Timothy McVeigh? These are questions of proportionality, questions exposing the myth that only the worst-of-the-worst get the ultimate punishment.

❖ *Something is amiss when a government that does not adequately deliver the mail delivers death sentences to some of its citizens.*

~MICHAEL A. MELLO

✑ **3** ☙

Finding Common Ground

 Far Away, a play by Caryl Churchill (London, 2000)

Caryl Churchill's chilling play is set in a futuristic totalitarian state, in which everything and everyone is at war. Not only nationalities (Moroccans, Canadians, Japanese, and Latvians), but groups of people (musicians, computer programmers, dentists, girls by the side of the road), animals, insects, and elements of nature (the grass, the rivers, light, dark, even gravity itself) have chosen sides. Everything has been "recruited" to one side or the other, although no disagreement is ever articulated: it seems to be beside the point.

The centerpiece of the drama is a grotesque parody of the Easter Parade, in which people condemned to death are presented before a panel of judges. Each of the condemned is wearing a number on their prison grays, a look of utter defeat, and a fantastical, Dr. Seuss-style hat, one more outlandish than the next—with bangles, ridiculous feathers, and loops of beads. Row after row of the hatted condemned march onto the stage as the audience grimaces, subjected to uncomfortably loud, upbeat, military march music.

Later, at her workbench, one of the hatmakers laments that it seems such a waste, after so much creativity and time has been put into their creation, to burn the hats with the bodies of the executed. Such a waste. Such a waste.

Common Ground: We All Want to Be Safe

Life in the United States of America is so much easier when we can pretend that there are only two positions to take on any given question, that somehow we all fit neatly into a "for" or "against." Like other oversimplified dualities—black or white, young or old, male or female, gay or straight, heaven or hell—our attitudes and beliefs are often more complex than politicians or reporters can handle in one sound bite.

On the subject of capital punishment, we are pitted against each other as if we were either "tough on crime" and on the side of the victims, or we are "soft on crime" and care only about the victimizers, the criminals themselves. People who are opposed to capital punishment are often accused of being oblivious to the feelings of crime victims, indulgent toward the accused, and overly protective of the rights of people in prison. There is an assumption that one might be so distracted by concerns for the accused that the problem of crime is ignored.

If we are ever to make progress in the death penalty debate, it is crucial that we state the obvious: No one is in favor of more crime. We all want to feel safe, in our homes, on our streets, in our cars, on the subway, at a ball game, in our churches, at a party, in a restaurant.

We want to feel safe, but night after night on the television news and in our entertaining crime dramas and movies, we are reminded that we are not safe. Little girls are kidnapped right out of their own beds. Little boys are abused by priests. Wives are beaten by husbands. The elderly are vulnerable to abusive attendants. Carjackers lurk at the mall. Snipers lurk in the shadows.

Now, there are terrorists. We eye each other with new suspicion, leave our backpacks home as we head into stadiums and remove our shoes, when asked, at the airport. Everything changed for us on September 11, 2001, as we are repeatedly reminded.

One thing, however, has not changed, and that is that we all want to be safe. Norman Rockwell was known for his mid-20th century depictions of *The Four Freedoms*. In the painting entitled *Freedom from Fear*, Rockwell depicted two parents tucking their children into bed. The once-popular World War II–era painting exudes an air of security, peace, comfort, safety, protection, the care and nurture of loving parents who will always be there.

It is fair to say that, even in this age of extreme sports, consensual power-and-pain games in the sexual arena, and daredevil TV shows like "Survivor" and "Fear Factor," in truth, we still long to live where we know ourselves to be safe and free from fear.

This is our first point of common ground: no one is on the side of crime. We all want to find answers. We want to feel safe to live our lives.

Common Ground: We Want Our Criminal Justice System to Be Fair

Just as those for capital punishment often act as if they are the only ones who are against crime, so those opposed often act as if they are the only ones who want the criminal justice system to be fair.

The national dialogue would be enhanced if we would assume that no one actually wants a system where the rich can buy pardons and the poor are targeted and trapped. For the sake of the victims of crime and their families and for the accused and their families, we do not want a system of deals for the slick and savvy or a rush to judgment. We do not want a system that leaves the real culprits out on the streets while others languish in cages for crimes they did not actually commit.

Let us agree that no one wants a broken system. We do not want a system that is arbitrary and inconsistent. We do not want a system that perpetuates the problems of our society.

This is the territory, however slim, of common ground. We share a desire for a system that is fair.

When George Ryan was elected Governor of Illinois, he thought his state had a fair system. A tough "law and order" Republican, he not only believed in the death penalty, he preached it with a passion. He was a true believer.

But the criminal justice system in his state, as in other states, is like a malfunctioning oversized bulldozer on the loose. A mammoth government program out of control, it rolled over guilty and innocent alike. The steering mechanism was nonfunctional. Someone had to stop it. Governor Ryan called a halt to all executions, a moratorium, hoping that he could fix what was broken and get the bulldozer back on the right track. He tried to overhaul the monster machine, urging state lawmakers to fix what was broken. Three times, the changes his commission proposed were rejected. Governor Ryan still believed in the death penalty; he just wanted it to be a fair system, a working system.

BASIC DEATH ROW RECIPE

(Notions of complexity and mercy have been removed,
making this recipe easy enough for beginners!
Lethal chemicals may be prepared in advance.)

Ingredients:
– sustained period of poverty or near poverty
– lifetime of chaos, steeped in any combination of the following:

drug addiction	physical/sexual abuse
rage	broken ties
mental illness	lack of education and/or
lack of social services	employment

– black skin or brown (victim should have white skin)
– bad luck
– violent crime if evidence is not available, mere accusation would
  be sufficient
– quick pinch of court-appointed lawyer (preferably inexperienced or incompetent, or both)

Combine the above ingredients and let sit, unattended, in a cold,
hard time and place. Heap on hot and spicy taunts by uninformed
radio talk show personalities and tough nuggets of raw verbiage
by politicians running for office. (WARNING: may cause bloating
of budgets, shortage of resources, numbness of sensibilities, and
hardening of hearts.)

As mentioned in the previous chapter, days before he left office, in
January of 2003, Governor Ryan stunned the nation. With the massive
program still broken, he went one step beyond moratorium and reform.
He shut down the Illinois death row by commuting the sentences of
163 men and four women to long prison terms or life. Further, he
granted full pardons to four men because their confessions had been
coerced by use of torture in a notorious Chicago police station.

He said, "The Legislature couldn't reform it, lawmakers won't repeal it, and I won't stand for it. I must act." Knowing he risked the outrage of many, the Governor said he was determined to take this drastic action, "because our three-year study has found only more questions about the fairness of the sentencing, because of the spectacular failure to reform the system, because we have seen justice delayed for countless death row inmates with potentially meritorious claims, because the Illinois death penalty system is arbitrary and capricious—and therefore immoral."

The desire to fix what is broken, to make the system fair, is a daunting feat, as Governor Ryan discovered. Where do we begin to unravel what is wrong? It is a tangled skein of interwoven threads. Grab just one thread—say, for example, the right to legal counsel. That thread is tied to the issue of access, which is knotted to an issue of funding and availability of law books, which is tied to funding again, and prison libraries (or lack thereof) and issues of literacy . . . and we have an impossible tangle.

Try again. Grab the thread of crime control, which leads backward toward issues of law enforcement, drug trafficking, drug rehabilitation, prevention, education and opportunity (or lack thereof), despair. The same thread leads forward toward issues of sentencing, judicial discretion, privatization of the prisons, prison overcrowding, lack of opportunity post-release. . . . Again, the threads are too tangled, each leading to other seemingly unsolvable problems.

And so we narrow the field, because the whole thing is just too much—too damaged, out of control, beyond our capacity to imagine significant change. This kind of complexity requires a vast overhaul, but we're stuck pulling bits of thread from the tangled mess.

📺 TV show from the series "Sliders"—*Dead Man Sliding* by Nan Hagan, original air date, November 29, 1996

In "Sliders," the four lead characters slide through a portal that delivers them to a different parallel universe each week.

In this episode, the four land on a world where criminal trials are conducted as game shows. The people of this Earth have become frustrated with lengthy trials, seemingly endless appeals, thorny issues of guilt and innocence, and the high cost to taxpayers. They have tossed out the entire system in favor of a game show.

Within minutes of landing, Quinn, the show's main character, becomes a victim of mistaken identity. He is arrested and made to stand before the audience, which, with no evidence and little provocation, begins to chant, "Guilty! Guilty! Guilty!" After a hasty vote on the verdict, Quinn is given a choice of doors to open. He hesitates, forfeiting his "choice." In game-show fashion, a flashing, blinking wheel is spun around until its pointer stops on door number two, behind which is the instrument of death: a guillotine. The crowd goes wild. The sentence will be carried out the next evening.

Professor Arturo, one of the Sliders, laments, "This world is only interested in entertainment. They don't give a damn about the truth."

Seven Ways in which
the Death Penalty Is Routinely Unfair

(1) The death penalty has been imposed on people whose innocence was still open to debate

In recent years, public opinion has radically shifted toward a moratorium on the death penalty, as a parade of wrongly convicted inmates has been freed from death row.

When George Ryan, once known as a "heartland conservative," made his famous speech in January, 2003, effectively emptying out the death row cells of Illinois, he publicly reviewed the case that had turned him around 180 degrees. He said,

> I never intended to be an activist on this issue, needless to say. Soon after taking office I watched in surprise and amazement as freed death row inmate Anthony Porter was released from jail. As a free man, he ran into Northwestern University Professor Dave Protess—where's David?—It was a memory I'll never forget, seeing little Anthony Porter run into your arms as a free man. He poured his heart and soul, David did, into proving Porter's innocence with his journalism students.
>
> Anthony Porter was 48 hours away from being wheeled into the execution chamber, where the state would kill him.
>
> It would all be so antiseptic, and most of us would not have even paused, except that Anthony Porter was innocent. He was innocent of the double murder for which he had been condemned to die.

And after Mr. Porter's case there was a report by *Chicago Tribune* reporters Steve Mills and Ken Armstrong that documented the systemic failures of our capital punishment system. And you've all read it. I can't imagine: half, half, if you will, of the nearly 300 capital cases in Illinois had been reversed for a new trial or re-sentencing. How many of you here today who are professionals can get by with 50 percent accuracy? . . .

How does that happen? How in God's name does that happen? In America, how does it happen? I've been asking this question for nearly three years and so far nobody's answered this question.

Then over the next few months, there were three more exonerated men, freed because their sentence hinged on a jailhouse informant, or new DNA technology proved beyond a shadow of a doubt their innocence . . .

If you really want to know what's outrageous and unconscionable, seventeen exonerated death row inmates is nothing short of a catastrophic failure. . . .

Our capital system is haunted by the demon of error: error in determining guilt, and error in determining who among the guilty deserves to die. Because of all of these reasons, today I am commuting the sentences of all death row inmates.

(More from this speech can be found in Appendix 1)

Anthony Porter, a man with an IQ of only 51, had been phenomenally lucky after eighteen years of bad luck. New evidence had been found—not by law-enforcement people or lawyers—but by university students completing a class assignment. Because of their diligence, not only was Porter freed, but the real killer was found. Interrogated by a detective, he confessed to the crime.

Governor Ryan let himself be completely shocked that an innocent man had come so close to being executed. He said, "I felt jolted into reexamining everything I believed in."

❖ *As to the fact that the death penalty ensnares innocent Americans in its complicated legal web: Since 1976, more than 100 people have been freed from Death Row due to actual innocence, while close to 800 people have been executed. That means that for every eight people we are executing, one person is completely exonerated. What if a prescription drug cured eight of every nine people who took it, but killed the ninth? What if an airline carrier successfully completed eight of every nine flights it launched, but the ninth resulted in mechanical failure? What if you were able to reboot your computer successfully eight out of nine tries, but every ninth time it crashed and destroyed your work? As a society that depends upon a functioning criminal justice system, can we have confidence when that same justice system sends innocent people to Death Row?*

~ STEVEN W. HAWKINS

It is possible, in the United States, to be put to death while large questions about one's guilt or innocence remain unanswered. Indeed, innocence is sometimes deemed irrelevant.

Joseph O'Dell was sentenced to death in Virginia and was stymied by that state's brief twenty-one-day limit on evidence which comes to light after a conviction. When O'Dell heard about DNA testing, not available at the time of his conviction, he was sure he could be exonerated by the new technology. The system that sent him to his execution in 1997 didn't care one way or the other. Maybe he was innocent. Maybe he was guilty. His request—that the crime scene evidence be tested for his DNA—was rejected. Remarkably, the reason given by Attorney General Mary Sue Terry was that, "Evidence of innocence is irrelevant."

❖ *When state officials have no qualms about executing people even though there are clear doubts about their guilt and about whether they have been treated fairly by the justice system, it's time to bring the curtain down on their ability to execute anyone.*

~ BOB HERBERT

Roger Keith Coleman was executed in Virginia in 1992 though questions about his innocence remained unanswered. A coal miner, he had been convicted of murdering his sister-in-law on circumstantial evidence and the testimony of a jailhouse informant, who later recanted. The prosecutors withheld evidence that did not support their case. Coleman was denied a crucial appeal because his inexperienced, court-appointed lawyers missed the filing deadline by mere hours. They had sent the papers by regular mail, and the package was delivered late. The appeal was thus deemed "procedurally defaulted," and Coleman was executed.

That same year, in the state of Texas, Leonel Herrera cried out, "I am innocent, innocent, innocent. . . . Something very wrong is happening here," as he was about to be executed, despite evidence of innocence. When the Supreme Court voted 6–3 that his likely innocence was not reason enough to intervene in the state's process, the three dissenting justices protested, "The execution of a person that can show he is innocent comes perilously close to simple murder." *Perilously close?*

> ❖ *The calculated killing of a human being by the state involves, by its very nature, an absolute denial of the executed person's humanity. The most vile murder does not, in my view, release the state from constitutional restraints on the destruction of human dignity. Yet an executed person has lost the very right to have rights, now or ever.*
>
> *For me, then, the fatal constitutional infirmity of capital punishment is that it treats members of the human race as nonhumans, as objects to be toyed with and discarded. It is indeed "cruel and unusual." It is thus inconsistent with the fundamental premise of the Constitution that even the most base criminal remains a human being possessed of some potential, at least, for common human dignity.*
>
> ~SUPREME COURT JUSTICE WILLIAM BRENNAN

Innocents sentenced to death have made for compelling theater since Victor Hugo (1802–85) wrote *The Hunchback of Notre Dame*. Set in medieval Paris, it is, in part, the story of the grotesque but big-hearted bell-ringer, Quasimodo, who rescues the innocent, enchanting Gypsy girl, Esmerelda, from public execution.

At the other end of the dramatic spectrum, but no less compelling, is the documentary play, *The Exonerated* (New York, 2002) by Jessica Blank and Erik Jensen. Staged with dignified spareness as a concert reading, the script is based on edited interviews with six former death row prisoners who were eventually found to be innocent. Woven into the tapestry of voices are those of the arresting officers, lawyers, and family members of the wrongfully imprisoned. The stories of those exonerated, told in their own words—of interrogation, arrest, trial, and imprisonment—are harrowing. They are the words of people whose lives were suddenly caught in the relentless gears of the bone-crushing criminal justice machine. One character looks at the audience and says, "I'll give you a moment just to reflect. From 1976 to 1992 [the years of her incarceration for a crime she did not commit], just remove that entire chunk from your life."

(2) The death penalty is a system plagued by racism

> ❖ *The death penalty is a direct descendant of lynching and other forms of racial violence and racial oppression in America.*
>
> ~STEPHEN B. BRIGHT

Racism is inherent in our criminal justice system. Its ugly reality is as obvious as the flashy necktie worn by a Louisiana attorney to the courtroom several times in late 2002. The tie got attention, not only because it was bright red, but because it featured a six-inch noose as its main design. As reported in the *New York Times*, the tie's significance was not lost on Lawrence Jacobs, Jr., the young black man on trial for murder in the predominately white New Orleans suburb. The point was driven home when an assistant district attorney whispered in his ear, "We're going to hang you, boy."

> ❖ *The U.S. prison system has always had an apartheid character, writes philosopher C. George Caffentzis. Especially after the Civil War and the announced abolition of slavery, the prisons became the major locus for the continual enforcement of slave conditions for black Americans. In short, today's prisons are enmeshed in the legacy of slavery just as today's capital punishment is in the legacy of lynching.*
>
> ~MARK LEWIS TAYLOR

There are two basic ways in which racism impacts our system of capital punishment. First, in the United States, the murder of a white person is taken more seriously than the murder of a person of color. Even though more than half of the victims of homicide are people of color, approximately eight out of ten people on death row are there for killing a white person. Sister Helen Prejean has said of this statistic, "You look at the history of racism in this country: it has always been considered the most terrible offense to commit a crime against a white person, or white people's property. In reverse we see that when people of color are killed, there is often a shrug of the shoulders and indifference."

> ❖ *Other than wealth, the most salient factor in the death penalty system in America is race. Over seventeen thousand executions have occurred in the United States. Of that number, a total of thirty-five have involved a white murderer and a black victim.*
>
> ~DAVID R. DOW

Second, crimes by people of color are punished more harshly than crimes by white people. Some 2.1 million people are incarcerated in the United States. Although African Americans are approximately thirteen percent of the nation's population, they make up more than forty-three percent of the general prison population. As we begin the 21ˢᵗ century, there are approximately thirty-five hundred prisoners on death row in the United States. Forty-one percent are black.

❖ *The death penalty symbolizes whom we fear and don't fear, whom we care about and whose lives are not valid.*
~BRYAN STEVENSON

In 1972, the Supreme Court, in *Furman v. Georgia*, held that the death penalty was unconstitutional specifically because it was deemed discriminatory and arbitrary. For four years, the death penalty came to a halt in the United States while lawmakers scrambled to fix it. In 1976, with *Gregg v. Georgia*, the Supreme Court seemed convinced that states had managed to iron out the problems. Today, those who defend capital punishment overlook or dismiss the varieties of racism in law enforcement and throughout the judicial system, as though two hundred years of racial prejudice in the United States could be magically banished from this segment of our society.

❖ *Beyond any reasonable doubt, the US death penalty continues to reflect the deeply-rooted prejudices of the society that condones its use. Amnesty International cannot find any evidence that current legal safeguards eliminate racial bias in the application of the death penalty.*
~AMNESTY INTERNATIONAL REPORT

In his book, *Last Rights: 13 Fatal Encounters with the State's Justice,* United Church of Christ minister Joseph B. Ingle described the life and final days of Willie Darden, a black man executed in Florida on March 15, 1988. Darden had grown up in Greene County, North Carolina, in the 1930s, when blacks constituted half the total population but owned only four percent of the state's taxable wealth. He attended Sunday school every week and completed the eighth grade at the Zechariah School for the Colored and helped his grandfather homestead a "two-horse" farm.

Life changed for Darden when his beloved grandfather died and his stepmother deserted the family. Placed in foster care, Darden was forced to steal food and clothing to live. At age sixteen, he was sent to a segregated juvenile correctional facility. When he was released, opportunities for employment or education were scarce. He got married in 1955. One year later he was arrested for trying to cash a $48 forged check—to buy food. At some point, it seems, Darden gave up on his pursuit of a fulfilling life, meaningful employment, dreams of fairness in the segregated South. In and out of prison for convictions of forgery, theft, and assault, even menial jobs seemed beyond his reach. All he learned was the art of surviving prison life.

On September 8, 1973, Darden's car broke down outside of Christine Bass's house in Lakeland, Florida. Bass let Darden call a tow truck from her house, then watched as the man waited by his car. Around the same time, a white man was killed by a black man during a robbery of a furniture store, half-an-hour up the road. Willie Darden was later arrested for the crime.

Christine Bass tried to tell her story, and did, to anyone who would listen. Unfortunately, no one associated with the trial was interested in her testimony. As Joseph Ingle described it, "Willie's was the only black face in the courtroom. There was a white prosecutor, a white judge, a white defense lawyer, and an all-white jury. 'Joe,' Willie told me, 'when I looked around at all those white faces, I knew how it was gonna come out!'" Years later, Supreme Court Justice Harry Blackmun would say, "If ever a man received an unfair trial, Darden did. He may be guilty, I don't know, but he got a runaround in that courtroom."

During years of appeals, death warrants, and last minute stays, Bass tried to get someone to listen to her. She knew that Darden could not be guilty. Her testimony was finally entered into the record and was instrumental in staying one death warrant. Amnesty International publicized Darden's case. Although it remained of little interest in the United States, pleas to stop the execution came from around the world. Despite the appeals, the new governor of Florida signed a final death warrant. Strapped into the electric chair on the morning of March 15, 1988, Darden spoke his last words.

> I say to my friends and supporters around the world, I love each and every one of you. Your love and support have been a great comfort to me in my struggle for justice and freedom.

(3) The death penalty disproportionately affects the poor

Occasionally, we find one thread that dominates the tangled mess called capital punishment. Take, for example, the thread of poverty. It runs from the beginning of the tangle to the end and back again. It is connected to everything. As Sister Prejean bluntly stated in an interview with Fellowship of Reconciliation's executive director, John Dear, "Poverty? The death penalty is riddled with poverty. Only poor people are on death row. . . ." According to a recent report by Amnesty International, "Ninety-five percent of death row inmates cannot afford their own attorney."

> ❖ *Every person on death row in America lacks the resources to hire a dream team. Those who are charged with capital murder in jurisdictions that lack a public defender system are represented by lawyers who have been disciplined by the bar association at a rate five times greater than the norm.*
>
> ~DAVID R. DOW

Bettie Lou Beets didn't have money, or anyone to help her the first time she was raped, at age five, by her father, or throughout the years of physical, sexual, and emotional abuse that followed. She did not have money or anyone to help her when she dropped out of school in the seventh grade. She did not have money or anyone to help her when she was beaten by a string of husbands. She did not even have the term "battered woman" when it might have helped explain in court why she finally murdered her last chronic abuser. Her lawyer didn't mention her lifetime of abuse to the jury.

She submitted an essay for the February–May, 1990, issue of *Endeavor*, a newsletter by Texas death row inmates. In it, she wrote:

> I don't think one could ever say they are ready to die, that they are just ready to give up. There is always something you want to do, one more thank you want to say, one more point you want to make. . . .
>
> When I went back to court in August to be given a date of execution, as I was leaving the courthouse, my thoughts were these: Looking over the people in the courthouse. . . . I had to think of the woman in the Bible, the woman whom the people had carried into the city to be stoned to death. Jesus was there (as He was with me) and He was told why the woman was there and what she had done. Jesus looked down at the woman as if to say some unheard words. Some think He may have been saying "Where is the man?" He said to the people, "He who is without sin cast the first stone,"

and when He looked up all the people were gone. I thought of myself as that woman, and as I looked out at the people, I had to wonder, did they think they were without sin? Could it be they did not hear God's words, or could it be they were just curious? Well, we may never know for sure, but I don't think they were thinking of that woman at all.

Although some battered women kill their abusers, are arrested, serve time, and get out to start new lives, Bettie Lou Beets, a great grandmother, was executed at the age of 62 in Huntsville, Texas on February 24, 2000.

❖ *Little wonder that capital sentences continue to be meted out almost exclusively to the poor and deprived, social outcasts and pariahs, the products of ghetto schools that did not teach and of reform schools that did not*

By permission of the artist, Gary Donatelli

reform, and of all of the other failings of our affluent society which can spend millions for capital prosecution but begrudges pennies for adequate childcare or nutrition or mental health care or decent schooling for today's children of poverty who will be tomorrow's death row inmates.

~ANTHONY AMSTERDAM

(4) The death penalty disproportionately affects those with mediocre legal representation

❖ *The Constitution says that everyone's entitled to an attorney of their choice. But the Constitution does not say that the lawyer has to be awake.*
~JUDGE DOUG SHAVER, TEXAS DISTRICT COURT

In the United States, a person can be sentenced to death even if their lawyer sleeps through the trial. In 1995, Carl Johnson was executed in Texas, even though his lawyer had been asleep during portions of the jury selection and parts of the trial.

Houston Chronicle reporter John Makeig covered the capital trial of George McFarland, observing, "Seated beside his client . . . defense attorney John Benn spent much of Thursday afternoon's trial in apparent deep sleep. His mouth kept falling open and his head lolled back on his shoulders, and then he awakened just long enough to catch himself and sit upright. Then it happened again. And again. And again."

❖ *Capital punishment is a lottery, but it is a rigged lottery, skewed by matters of politics, class, race, geography and, most importantly, the quality and resources of the defense lawyer at trial.*
~MICHAEL A. MELLO

Calvin J. Burdine's lawyer also slept through significant portions of his 1983 trial. The trial lasted only six days and concluded with his sleepy lawyer having only five pages of handwritten notes. Burdine, who is gay, was referred to in derogatory terms by both his own lawyer and by the prosecutor who urged the imposition of the death penalty, because, "sending a homosexual to the penitentiary certainly isn't a very bad punishment for a homosexual." Burdine's biased lawyer never objected. In 2002, after nineteen years on death row, Burdine got lucky: the Supreme Court ruled that he was entitled to a new trial.

❖ *The death penalty is a rotten edifice, and you will find terrible problems no matter where you look.*
   Lying witnesses. Lousy lawyers. Corrupt prosecutors. Racism.
   The death penalty is broken and can't be fixed. Get rid of it.
                                                    ~BOB HERBERT

Aden Harrison, Jr., an African American, was represented by an 83-year-old court-appointed lawyer who had been an Imperial Wizard of the Ku Klux Klan for more than fifteen years.

❖ *In Kentucky, an attorney [in a capital case] who gave his business address as Kelly's Keg, the local watering hole, was assigned to a capital case. He had no experience. His home was decorated with a big neon beer sign. He missed the testimony of important witnesses because he was out of the courtroom. He came to the trial drunk. When police searched his home, they found garbage bags hidden under a floor containing stolen property. The court said that his behavior did not adversely affect his client.*

   ~BARRY SCHECK, PETER NEUFELD, JIM DWYER

Judy Haney's court-appointed attorney was drunk during some portions of the 1989 capital trial, so drunk, in fact, that the lawyer was held in contempt and sent to jail, only to be released the next day to resume trial.

❖ *People who are well represented at trial do not get the death penalty. I have yet to see a death penalty case among the dozens coming to the Supreme Court on eve-of-execution stay applications in which the defendant was well represented at trial.*

   ~SUPREME COURT JUSTICE RUTH GINSBURG

Even when a lawyer is competent and attempting to provide fair representation for the accused, the system itself can defeat the best intentions, as noted in this anecdote:

❖ *In one of my first cases, I was putting the finishing touches on a motion for a stay of execution, when I received over the fax machine an order from the court denying the motion. In another case, the court of appeals claimed to have reviewed the entire record before denying the motion, even though the record never entered the chambers of the judge who wrote the order.*

Every death penalty lawyer has many such stories, because these stories are not unique.

~DAVID R. DOW

(5) The death penalty has been inflicted on the retarded

While on the campaign trail for the presidency in 1992, Governor Bill Clinton took time out from his hectic schedule to oversee the execution of Rickey Ray Rector in Arkansas. Rector was brain damaged. He could not tell time, nor could he understand his own dire situation. As he was led to the execution chamber, he asked the guards to save part of his last meal—a piece of pecan pie—for later. While strapped to the gurney, he tried to help his executioners find a good vein for them to insert the IV. It took fifty minutes.

❖ *There's Jerome Holloway, here in Georgia. Jerome has an IQ of 49, a mental age of a two-year-old. I did a test on Jerome and the same test on the two-year-old daughter of a colleague. She did much better than Jerome. He has no idea what's going on.*

~CLIVE STAFFORD-SMITH

Claiming that standards of decency had evolved in the United States, in June, 2002, the Supreme Court cited "national consensus" as its reason for ruling that the execution of people with mental retardation violates the Constitution. Unfortunately, the Court did not define mental retardation. Two weeks after the landmark ruling, the state of Texas reviewed the case of Johnny Paul Penry.

Penry's childhood of abuse is well documented. As an infant he was beaten by his mother who used her fists, mops, belts, extension cords, and boards. Once she tried to drown him in the bathtub. He was forced to eat his feces and drink his urine. Often he was locked up and left alone for long stretches. Neighbors heard terrible screams. Nothing was done. He never finished the first grade. By the time Penry was ten, he was diagnosed as retarded and brain damaged from repeated trauma. When Penry was in his early twenties, he crossed the line from sad little victim to monstrous victimizer and was convicted of committing a gruesome crime.

A long-time resident of the Texas death row, Penry spends his days coloring with crayons. He cannot read. He believes in Santa Claus.

Penry's IQ has consistently tested in the 50-to-63 range. An IQ of 70 is generally considered the threshold of mental retardation.

In an effort to get around the new ban on executing the retarded, Texas ruled that Penry was not really developmentally disabled after all and was, therefore, still eligible for execution in that state. In an interview with the *Houston Chronicle*, Governor Rick Perry dismissed the "national consensus" cited in the June, 2002, Supreme Court ruling. "The justice system in the state of Texas is basically for Texans," he said. Amnesty International issued a statement which read, "Texas has been pursuing the execution of John Penry for over two decades. It is difficult to view the state's apparent need to kill this man as anything but vengeance."

In March, 2003, as a new appeal was being prepared, a state judge removed Penry's lawyer, John Wright, from the case, although Wright had faithfully represented Penry for over two decades. The judge replaced Wright with a lawyer who originally assisted in Penry's prosecution. As this book goes to press, the saga continues.

(6) The death penalty has been inflicted on the mentally ill

In December, 1999, on the eve of his execution in Texas, David Long tried to commit suicide by overdosing on antipsychotic drugs. He was rushed to a hospital and placed on life support. Once he was stabilized, the state chartered a plane staffed with medical personnel and had him flown back to Huntsville where he was executed the following day.

> ❖ *There is no question about the insanity of the clients. They are really sick in very different ways. One is a coprophiliac; last year he was found licking out the inside of the toilet bowl. Toilet bowls are nasty, but can you imagine how bad they are in prison? . . . He has done incredibly brutal things to himself . . . He vacillates and is apparently quite bright, which makes it even more pathetic. It took me forever to get the authorities here to recognize that he was nuts, and this is in enlightened California where things are better than most states . . . The officials do not want to recognize that he's insane because if they do, and they get to the stage of strapping him in the gas chamber, that might present a real problem. So they pretend he's normal. That is insane!*
>
> ~ROBERT R. BRYAN

In 1986, the Supreme Court ruled, in *Ford v. Wainwright*, that the Constitution bars execution of an insane person. Unfortunately, the justices were vague about what constitutes insanity.

The story of Larry Robison is usually told from his mother's point of view. She had tried for years to get help for her troubled son. Larry had been a happy child, active in the Boy Scouts and Sunday School, often earning straight A's in school. At age twelve, everything changed. He became increasingly disturbed and started experimenting with drugs.

Lois Robison sought help as her son's behavior grew increasingly bizarre, but the family had no medical insurance and no hospital would keep him. He slipped through every crack in the system. Lois Robison, a third-grade schoolteacher, did not give up as she watched her son struggle with hallucinations.

He was diagnosed as a paranoid schizophrenic at age twenty-one. Still, professional help and medication remained out of his reach. Sometimes he was turned away for lack of money and insurance. Other times, the family was told that "budget considerations" prevented the various agencies from assisting Larry, who was showing increasingly severe signs of psychosis.

One day in 1982, he committed his first and only act of violence— the murder of five people. It was what his mother had been fearing for years.

Suddenly, the state of Texas found the money needed to keep Larry under 24-hour supervision—on death row. He was put to death on January 21, 2000, with lethal drugs costing Texas $86.08.

Alexander Williams, who suffered from chronic paranoid schizophrenia, was on death row for many years in Georgia. His problems dated from childhood when Williams was frequently thrown out of his house naked, beaten with a hammer, and often denied food and the use of the bathroom. None of this was mentioned by his attorney at his 1986 trial for a crime he committed when he was only seventeen. As his execution date neared, his case made headlines: helmeted prison officials were forcibly medicating Williams in order to make him sane enough for execution. On February 25, 2002, following a last-minute stay of execution, Williams's sentence was commuted to life in prison. The following November, he was found dead in his cell—an apparent suicide.

On March 26, 2003, James Colburn was executed in Texas. Diagnosed with acute paranoid schizophrenia while a teenager, his hallucinations and delusions got worse when he was raped. He turned to drugs and began to develop an arrest record. Hospitals would no longer provide treatment after his insurance coverage ended when he turned eighteen. He was actively psychotic when he killed Peggy Murphy in 1994. During his trial, he was given such high doses of the antipsychotic drug Haldol, that he slept through most of the proceedings.

David Funchess was awarded five medals for bravery in Vietnam, which is where he became addicted to drugs and was badly wounded in a land-mine explosion. When he returned to the States, he could not sleep because of nightmares. He spent his afternoons digging foxholes behind houses in a rundown neighborhood and entered his home carrying an imaginary machine gun in front of him. He was tried for murder in 1974, before post-traumatic stress disorder was recognized as a mitigating circumstance, and was executed on April 22, 1986.

Manny Babbitt was another mentally ill Vietnam veteran who wound up on death row. As a child, he had struggled with extreme poverty and severe learning disabilities. By the age of seventeen, he had only made it to the seventh grade. He gave up on schooling and, the following year, joined the Marines after a recruiter "helped" him with the exam.

Babbitt was only in Vietnam a month when the remote fire base where he was stationed came under siege in what would be the longest and bloodiest battle of the war. After fifty-six days of incessant action, Babbitt was struck in the head by rocket fragments.

Just as easily as he had been recruited, trained to kill, and shipped into a steamy, bewildering hell of battle, he was brought back and put on the streets, as if he could unlearn what he had picked up in training, as if he could just forget the fifty-six days of terror, of gunfire, screams, blood, and severed body parts. He could not. The visions continued for more than a decade as he battled post-traumatic stress disorder alone.

In 1980, during a delusional "flashback," he killed a 78-year-old Rumanian grandmother. His brother Bill brought Manny to the Sacramento police and authorities after they promised to get help for him. They broke their word. To Bill's horror, the full weight of the State was brought down on his disturbed brother. Manny was arrested, tried, and sentenced to death.

One person who understood Bill's torment and feeling of betrayal was David Kaczynski. With his wife Linda by his side, Kaczynski had approached the FBI in 1996, expressing his fear that his older brother Theodore—known in the media as the long-sought "Unabomber"— was responsible for the series of mail bombs that had killed three people and injured twenty-three over a period of seventeen years. Despite promises to the contrary, the Justice Department sought the death penalty, which was only overturned in a last-minute plea bargain.

Kaczynski lobbied unsuccessfully for clemency for Manny Babbitt, who was both poor and black. To the everlasting torment of his well-meaning brother Bill, Manny was executed on May 4, 1999, thirty-eight minutes after his fiftieth birthday.

More than three hundred mourners attended his funeral, which was followed by a graveside ceremony that included full military honors for the decorated Vietnam veteran. David Kaczynski, now serving as executive director of New Yorkers Against the Death Penalty, was one of the mourners. He said:

> Those of us who oppose the death penalty dream of a justice system that reflects what's best rather than what's worst in our national character. It's supposed to be blind to wealth and privilege, but it's anything but that. In effect, we've linked the impulse for revenge with a system that reflects the gamut of social inequalities. People are beginning to realize that this is a mockery of justice, and they're offended by it.

Louis Jones, a decorated Gulf War veteran, was executed on March 18, 2003, at the federal Penitentiary in Terre Haute, Indiana, just as the United States sent new troops into Iraq. He had served honorably for twenty-two years as an Army Airborne Ranger and retired as a Master Sergeant. According to an expert on illnesses related to the Gulf War, Jones had been in vigorous health when he went to Kuwait in January, 1991. There, as the Pentagon later confirmed, he had been exposed to nerve agents Sarin and Cyclosarin when the Army demolished a munitions plant in Khamisiyah, Iraq. A man with no criminal record, a long history of service, and with close family ties, Jones returned to the States in December, 1991, with brain damage and a change in his personality. Several years later, he kidnapped, raped and murdered Private Tracie McBride, a nineteen-year-old stationed at an Air Force Base in San Angelo, Texas. On the eve of his execution, his lawyer said in a statement:

The execution of Louis Jones represents the failure of the federal government to understand and be accountable for the impact of nerve agents on the soldiers who are exposed to it in the service of their country and on others who are affected by the damage done to those soldiers. It is a sad message that goes with our soldiers and their families—if you return from war damaged, the U.S. government won't take responsibility for that damage and its consequences.

(7) People convicted of capital crimes as juveniles can be executed in the United States

Since it is believed that the mind of an adolescent is less developed than the mind of an adult, and they are less able to handle social pressure, there is an almost universal prohibition on the execution of people who are under the age of eighteen when they committed their crime. According to Amnesty International, the United States and Somalia are the only countries that have refused to ratify the 1995 United Nations Convention on the Rights of the Child [Article 37 (a)] which states: "Neither capital punishment nor life imprisonment without possibility of release shall be imposed for offenses committed by persons below 18 years of age."

Amnesty International also claims that since 2000 only four countries in the world are known to have executed juveniles—the Democratic Republic of Congo, Iran, Pakistan, and the United States.

On May 28, 2002, the state of Texas executed Napoleon Beazley. Beazley had been president of his senior class and a football star in the East Texas town of Tyler. Then, at age seventeen, he and two friends attempted to steal a car and, in the process, Beazley shot and killed John Luttig, a civic leader and church elder. The black youth was sentenced to death by an all-white jury in Tyler. Nor was his case helped when the victim's son, a federal judge, moved his office from Virginia to Tyler where he routinely consulted with prosecutors. Despite international pressure, Beazley was put to death by lethal injection.

In November of that same year, Lee Malvo, age seventeen, was arrested with John Muhammad, age forty-one, for the sniper killings that had terrorized people in the Washington, D.C., area for three weeks. At the urging of Attorney General John Ashcroft, a fervent supporter of capital punishment, the Justice Department openly sought a jurisdiction that allows for the execution of juveniles. Maryland, where the majority of sniper killings took place, prohibits the execution of those younger than eighteen, so Malvo will be tried in Virginia. As this book goes to press, Malvo, whose mother reportedly "gave" him to John Muhammad as collateral for forged immigration papers, awaits trial in solitary confinement at the Fairfax County Adult Detention Center.

It matters that the most vulnerable populations in our society—people of color, the poor, the young, the mentally ill or retarded—are also the ones who are the first to be chewed up and spit out by our criminal justice system. This shared concern is our common ground: *no one wants a system that is fundamentally unfair.*

⚜ 4 ⚜

Facing Complicated Truths

📺 TV show from the series "Babylon 5"—*Passing through Gethsemane* by J. Michael Straczynski, original air date, November 27, 1995

In a distant future, "death of personality" has replaced the death penalty. A "mindwipe" erases the personality of a person found guilty of a crime and replaces it with a new personality before returning the offender to some form of community service.

In this episode, Brother Edward is a good-hearted and likable monk who, early in the script, says that, for him, the core moment of Christianity was Jesus's long wait in the garden of Gethsemane, knowing that he would be arrested by the Romans in the morning and crucified. The monk wonders if he would have had the same courage.

Happy with a life of doing good work, strange things begin to happen to Brother Edward. First, he finds a black rose in a tote bag and then the words DEATH WALKS AMONG US *written in blood on his walls. He begins to have nightmarish visions.*

He confides in Brother Theo who investigates. They learn that Brother Edward was once the infamous serial murderer Charles Dexter, a.k.a. "The Black Rose Killer," found guilty and sentenced to "death of personality." Family members of his victims have discovered Dexter's new incarnation and are bent on seeking revenge. As a first step, they have hired a telepath to break the mindwipe and revive some images from the previous life.

Although Brother Edward can now remember, he has truly changed. Eager to atone for crimes he committed when he was Dexter, he finds the courage to wait, in a kneeling posture, for his vengeful pursuers. Later, his friends find him, battered and near death, and, beside themselves with grief, administer last rites before the brave monk dies.

A few weeks pass and a new monk is introduced to the order. He is immediately recognized as the leader of those who tortured Brother Edward. Afraid someone will want to avenge the beloved monk's death and that the cycle of violence will continue, Brother Theo pointedly steers the conversation toward forgiveness.

Revenge: It May Feel Good in the Moment, but There's Hell to Pay the Next Day

Whom do we feel like killing? Whom would we like to see suffer a slow, painful, gruesome death?

Before we hold up our placards proclaiming that every life on death row is sacred in the eyes of God, before we gush about the poor unloved lost souls sitting in the bleak isolation and harsh landscape of the American death row, before becoming all starry-eyed over the potential for good in the worst of us—we must face our own longings for revenge.

It is no wonder we are sometimes dismissed as so many fools on the hill, singing "Kum Ba Yah" with tears streaming down our faces.

There are days when the sanest, most forgiving among us think vengeful thoughts about some of modern life's most ordinary moments—busy days when we could "just kill" the pushy S.O.B. who butts in line at the supermarket, or the obnoxious lout who cuts us off in traffic. Too trivial?

How are we supposed to feel about the lab researchers who pour acid into the eyes of rabbits or drill holes in the skulls of conscious monkeys, or the man who finds it amusing to torment a circus elephant until the animal finally goes berserk, or the teenager who sets the cat on fire and laughs about it?

Isn't it normal to want revenge for such heartless deeds?

Who hasn't had a murderous or vengeful thought after seeing on the evening news a report about the live-in boyfriend who beat the teething baby to death or about the slum landlord, basking in the warmth of a Caribbean vacation, whose elderly tenant froze to death for lack of heat? Who didn't feel a murderous rage at the report that four adult men gang-raped an infant girl? Doesn't it just feel right to want them to suffer too?

What happens when such cruelty leaps from the front page of the newspaper and barges into our own homes like everybody's worst nightmare?

Whom do you want to kill? Whom could you imagine loathing unto death?

When ex-Governor Ryan appeared on "Oprah," in January, 2003, a camera panned the faces in the audience as they listened to details of one particularly gruesome multiple murder: two crazed people had broken into a house, shot a pregnant woman in the head, and, before the woman was actually dead, ripped open her abdomen and tore out her fully formed nine-month-old fetus, then tortured and killed the other children in the house. Ryan's blanket commutation of sentences had taken these murderers off death row and put them in prison for life. Audience members were in tears. They shook their heads in disbelief or stared at the stage with their mouths open. "But why remove *these* two from death row?" Oprah asked again and again.

There is something absolutely right about our outrage and contempt for the people who commit such crimes—even if we say that we hate the act and not the actor. It feels *right* to hate perverted, sadistic cowards, and yet, time and again, such hatred is dismissed by those who oppose the death penalty. And every time we dismiss this hatred, we seem smug, above the fray, and out-of-touch.

Part of the work we must do to be truly persuasive in our anti-death penalty work is the gritty, grimy work of getting our hands dirty with the raw side of crime, the utter torment of victimization. To so many it must look like we waltz in, long after the blood has been washed from the walls, after the screams of the victims have been stilled, after the years of silent heartache and loss have taken their toll on the bewildered loved ones left behind. Only then do we seem to appear on the scene, arms stretched wide to embrace—not the innocent victims!—but those convicted of the crimes.

One of the strengths of the movie *Dead Man Walking* is that the condemned man is not prettied up for us. We are forced to hear his racist, white-supremacist, sexist language and beliefs. We look hard at the swastika tatoo. We have to follow the well-meaning but very confused nun into the bathroom where she faces herself in the mirror crying, "My God, what am I doing?" In a crucial flashback, we watch the heartless and wildly horrifying crime unfold—the rape and murder of two lively, lovely young people. We have to work, watching that movie, to get to the place where we can walk down the stark, ugly hallway with the nun and the boy and the guards, see through the horror to the heart of the matter, and "be the face of love" for the condemned man at the moment of his death. It is a process. It is not pretty. It is not easy.

The lesson of the movie is precisely that it is hard work to "be the face of love." If we think it is easy, we have skipped a step, taken a shortcut, bypassed the mine field of human emotion. We are out of touch and ultimately, we will be ineffective in our work against capital punishment. We won't be credible. We won't be believable. In truth, we cannot get there from here—we cannot get to be the face of love, until we have done the hard work of facing our own impulse for revenge.

> ❖ *I tremble at the thought of how I might react if anyone killed my daughter or my son. I wouldn't be strong enough to control my anger and maybe I too would seek revenge. So I well understand the demand for revenge and compensation.*
>
> *But I also know that society must fight for something better than what we are in our worst moments. If we want the great promise of our civilization to come true—that is, a constant battle for greater justice—we can't base our law on this emotion.*
>
> ~MARIO CUOMO

To be effective, we must come to our position of being opposed to capital punishment, not because we are one hundred percent loving and forgiving, but in spite of the fact that we are not.

There are innocent people, alone and unloved, sitting in death row cages—but most of the people on death row are guilty. There are people there who are basically likable or talented, who have gotten in touch with their better selves during their long years of incarceration, or are childlike in their dementia, retardation, or mental illness—but some of the people on death row are simply sick, grinning bastards, people who really cannot be trusted ever to walk in freedom again; nasty perverts; warped; mean. This is part of the complicated truth that we must face to be effective.

❖ *Let me tell you about some neighbors on my block in Brooklyn. They have been dear friends for 15 years. They are good people, thinking people. They take progressive stands on most issues. They care about racial justice and economic justice. But the other day the conversation turned to the death penalty and they said, "Wait just a minute, this is where we draw the line." It was not that they were uninformed. They knew the death penalty doesn't deter crime. They knew it was cost ineffective. They knew that race played a pernicious role in its application. They knew that innocent people had been tragically executed. They knew all the talking points for all the talk show debates, yet they were dead set for the death penalty. And why you may ask? Why, in light of all this enlightenment? Revenge! They wanted revenge. They were sickened by the level and viciousness of crime in this country and they wanted revenge. And they are not alone. But somewhere along their journey we failed them. They had not been reached by the good news of the Gospel—the tough good news of the Gospel. . . .*

~ REVEREND DAVID DYSON

Actor-activist Danny Glover spoke against the death penalty in a handsome lecture hall at Princeton University on November 15, 2001, just two months after the 9/11 terrorist attack. All went well until the question-and-answer part of the presentation, when a man stood up and asked Glover whether he would be in favor of executing Osama bin Laden—if we could find him. Glover said he was opposed to all state executions, even Osama bin Laden's. There was a burst of angry muttering and movement as a number of people grabbed their coats and pushed their way through the crowded audience to the exit doors. Still raw in our minds' eyes were the images of men and women in business clothes leaping from the upper windows of the towers and of dead firemen, disintegrated to nothing more than ashes on the wind. Manhattan's mutilated skyline still had the power to shock. Pieces of charred invoices and spreadsheets remained stuck to the branches of our trees. We had seen a photograph which seemed to show the face of an evil, demented genie peering through the smoke. We had heard President George W. Bush call for bin Laden's capture—"dead or alive."

Was it a failure to express outrage or address a sympathetic urge toward revenge that made those audience members jump up and leave the room, as if their hearts were on fire with a burning rage that the rest of us could not feel? Did they feel invisible?

The point is not to deny our desire for revenge, but to get in touch with it and then, in spite of it, to oppose capital punishment. Even if we feel like killing sometimes, we don't want our basest feelings to become government policy. We don't want the state to act out of our need, however understandable, for revenge.

❖ *I don't want any person put to death in my name and with my money. It will always be the poor, the underclass, the mentally ill, and the mentally retarded who are executed. The death penalty institutionalizes vengeance, which is a natural emotion, but not one the state should be promoting.*

~DENISE GRAGG

Capital Punishment Impacts Those Who Impose It

❖ *I have heard all the arguments, analyzed all the evidence I could find, measured public opinion—when it was opposed, when it was indifferent, when it was passionately in favor. And always I have concluded that the death penalty is wrong: that it lowers us all; that it is surrender to the worst that is in us; that wielding the official power to kill by execution has never elevated a society, never made a single person safer, never brought back a life, never inspired anything but hate.*

~MARIO CUOMO

Executions are expensive. Counting everything that cannot be trimmed, they cost more than incarcerating a person for life. Capital trials have two separate phases—conviction and sentencing. According to Amnesty International, the greatest costs are incurred prior to and during the trials, not in post-conviction proceedings. In Florida, for example, each execution (from arrest to the final moment with the strap-down team) costs from two to three million dollars, compared to $600,000 for life imprisonment.

The death penalty eats up our resources while accomplishing nothing. With that money we could build schools and housing, parks and playgrounds; buy health coverage for our uninsured and drug rehabilitation for the addicted; provide literacy and job training for people trying to dig their way out of poverty. We get nothing for our money when it is spent on executions.

❖ *It is the deed that teaches, not the name we give it. Murder and capital punishment are not opposites that cancel one another, but similars that breed their kind.*

~GEORGE BERNARD SHAW

We learn a bad lesson from capital punishment. We learn that our government really does think killing works. When all else fails, it too turns to death as a tool. Every time we allow our government to put a citizen to death, we learn that killing is an acceptable option, an answer to a problem.

But more than that, executions eat our souls. One of my favorite buttons proclaims in bold letters: YOUR HATE BECOMES YOU. Hatred is like Janus, the two-faced Roman god of the gateway (after whom the month of January is named). One face of hatred looks back at the wrong that has been done. With this face we stare, as if mesmerized, at the facts of the crime, the blood and gore. We feed ourselves on the grisly details as if we can't get enough. And maybe we can't. Night after night we entertain ourselves with crime dramas on television—"Law and Order" and its many spin-offs or "N.Y.P.D. Blue." This week's episode will be about a woman "beaten to death with a drill."

Having looked back, time and again, at the stuff of past fear and hatred, we also look ahead, anticipating the fear and hatred in our future. In his award-winning 2002 documentary, *Bowling for Columbine*, Michael Moore exposed our obsession with fear, as if we want to scare ourselves to death with the possibility, however remote, of violence. We keep our own adrenalin pumping, arm ourselves to the teeth, put surveillance cameras at our entranceways and intersections, and elect politicians who boast of being tough on crime.

> ❖ *The need for revenge and the anger that accompanies it are a sickness of the soul that ultimately destroys the one who harbors them. Those who thirst for revenge may experience the illusion of satisfaction, but this never lasts long. For every act of violence leaves in its wake the seeds for more violence.*
>
> ~BROTHER BERNIE SPITZLEY

On one end of the spectrum, we find people who shrug in utter disinterest when a person is executed. In Huntsville, Texas, one diner has been known to sell a "Killer Burger" on execution days.

On the other end of the spectrum are people who turn up at the prison gates to cheer at an execution. Often, like unwitting clowns at a carnival of death, they are cavalier, contemptuous, and arrogant, drinking and laughing as if they were at a football rally. Their homemade signs feature clever puns or glib retorts.

The night serial killer Ted Bundy was executed in 1989, nearly three hundred people showed up to party. They waved signs that read, ROAST IN PEACE and THIS BUZZ IS FOR YOU, and THANK GOD IT'S FRY-DAY. When the execution was over, at shortly after 7 A.M., the crowd set off fireworks and cheered. At an earlier Florida execution, in 1985, seventy-five uniformed Jacksonville police officers popped champagne corks and lifted their glasses when cop-killer J. D. Raulerson was put to death.

Although they claim to speak for the victims, the people who show up to cheer executions rarely display any sense of the tragedy that befell the victims, choosing to voice, instead, only the call for vengeance.

Watching the sideshow, at the hour of death, it is apparent that capital punishment not only continues the cycle of violence, but serves to coarsen and numb our sensibilities. Some signs of the brutalizing effect of capital punishment are more obvious, albeit more bizarre, than others. In 2000, at a mall arcade in suburban Rockville, Maryland, thrill seekers, young and old, enjoyed an amusement ride called The Original Shocker. According to a published report by Rowan Philip,

> Some families went on picnics in the park at the weekend. And others watched their loved ones fry in the electric chair.
> Parents stood with uneasy grins as their children howled and jiggled on Ol' Sparky, the sound of electricity crackling in their ears and smoke rising over their heads. Wives zapped husbands with zeal. Teenagers shouted, "But I didn't do it!" before getting the juice . . .
> The Shocker comes with oversized oak throne, leather limb re-straints, and a numbing vibration system that seeks to simulate the "13,200 volts" threatened on the side.

Death Row Marv is another item of entertainment. Manufactured in 2000 by McFarlane Toys as part of the Sin City line, Marv is a square-jawed "action figure" that comes with a toy electric chair and wired helmet. Put Marv in the chair, throw the switch, and watch Marv twitch. As the chair makes a buzzing sound, Marv's eyes glow red, and he growls, "That the best you can do, you pansies?" Costing approximately $30, it is aimed at the fourteen-to-forty-five male market who would buy the doll primarily in comic book shops and music stores. The initial run "in the tens of thousands" sold out. Marv garnered international media headlines, from the *Times* of India (MACABRE MERRIMENT) to the *Australian* (DOLL MAKES EXECUTION CHILD'S PLAY).

These examples can rightly be said to belong in the realm of the extreme. Most of us probably would not buy our children a Death Row Marv doll. In truth, it is the more subtle effects of capital punishment that we should worry about.

❖ *I was doing some studies a few years ago on the French Revolution, and you see a momentum building up over the course of that revolution as they executed people. The more they executed, the more freedom they felt to execute, and the more of a bloodbath it became. If you really do a thorough study of the French Revolution, you see in it a growing callousness toward human life . . . it defies all logic to suppose that you can encourage the respect for human life through the device of taking human life. It's as simple as that.*

~PAUL KEVE

It is a truism that we become what we think. Thoughts and actions, repeated into routine, shape and define us—both as individuals and as a society. It is a truth as old as the Bible. In the Hebrew Scripture, Deuteronomy 30:19, it says, "I have set before you life and death, blessings and curses. Choose life so that you and your descendants may live."

❖ *Here on the surface of the world, we continue to flail around, chasing after our own worst instincts, until the world becomes a river of blood, a vicious cycle of blood lust, revenge and violence. Kosovo, Oklahoma City, Hilltop Drive, San Quentin.*

But far beneath the surface of the world there is an immutable law at work and that law says, life is sacred. All of life. Every life.

And that law says every human being is the bearer of the Divine, every human life is absolutely unique, absolutely precious.

And that law says it took all of time and all of eternity to produce every human life. And that law says that every human life is the potential source of a whole world full of subsequent lives, so that to kill a single human being is tantamount to killing a whole world. . . .

And that law is an immutable law and that law was there from the beginning of time and it will be there after time is over and that law says and that law will always say this: A million years will pass, the mountains will crumble and the rivers will run dry, but killing will never bring peace. Not once. It's a spiritual impossibility. Hatred and violence can only bring more hatred, more violence in their wake; horror, more horror. They can never bring peace. Only love can bring peace.

This is an immutable law. This is the law that runs beneath the surface of the world and has always run there.

~RABBI ALAN LEW

One compelling reason to oppose the death penalty is because we do not want to participate in murder. We do not want our lives, work, money, energy, or votes to be used for death. We do not want our society to make the same choice that a murderer makes—imposing death by killing.

One of the abolition movement's favorite bumper sticker and T-shirt slogans is the question: WHY DO WE KILL PEOPLE WHO KILL PEOPLE TO SHOW THAT KILLING PEOPLE IS WRONG? Activist and singer Holly Near turned this into an effective song entitled "Foolish Notion." It is a point of logic that has been expressed in many ways, by many people:

❖ *Our desire for justice, retribution, and even revenge comes to us naturally. But why let murderers debase our values and diminish our love for life? Why allow murderers to make us participants in perpetuating cycles of violence and revenge? Why drag all of us down by placing the blood of unnecessary killing on all of our hands?*

~REPRESENTATIVE CLIFTON C. BELOW

❖ *I have such a vindictive streak in me that I am surprised to find myself in opposition to the death penalty. Some days getting back at someone is the most fun I have and yet I do not approve of society putting anyone to death . . . When I was eight I was playing marbles with Buddy Duffey and he asked me if I had to kill either my mother or my father, which would I? I remember I refused to try and decide that and I feel the same way now about the death penalty. Being against the whole thing, I don't have to decide which method of execution is best. My objection to the death penalty doesn't come out of any sympathy I have for the murderers. What I object to is making a murderer of anyone else.*

~ANDREW A. ROONEY

❖ *Prior to my father's murder I had evolved a personal set of values that included a respect for life and an opposition to the death penalty.*

Although I am of the Irish-Catholic tradition, whose religious teachings include "Thou shalt not kill," that's not all of it; it is just more of how I want to live my life and the vision I have for the society I want to live in. For me to change my beliefs because my father was murdered would only give over more power to the killers, for they would take not just my father's life, but my values.

The same is true for society. If we let those who murder turn us to murder, it gives over more power to those who do evil. We become what we say we abhor.

~REPRESENTATIVE ROBERT RENNY CUSHING

❖ *The whole ritual in the death chamber was very fast. To me, what it said was that they take a living person, who took twenty-five years to create—and even Terry Roach, as damaged as he was, was unique, there never has been anyone like him and there never will be again, all of modern science cannot create his fingernail—and within just a few seconds they converted him into a piece of junk to be wrestled out on a stretcher and carted away. To me, the message was that human beings are junk and if you don't believe it—watch this. It is a completely incomprehensible miracle how a human being comes into this world, but to snuff one out is nothing. It is the easiest thing. Murderers can do it, anyone can do it. We can do it. Watch this! It was banal. That was my reaction, and it was hard to believe that there were people who knew him, who loved him, who at that moment were waiting with anguish, because he appeared to be just a piece of trash. It was dehumanizing. Not only to him. It was a ritual which denied the importance and uniqueness of any of us.*

~DAVID BRUCK

People Can Change

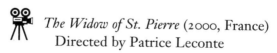 *The Widow of St. Pierre* (2000, France)
Directed by Patrice Leconte

After a night of drinking, two fishermen murder a man for the fun of it. Tried, sentenced to death, and driven through the streets, they make a rare sight on St. Pierre—a bleak, isolated island off the coast of Newfoundland. Feeling righteous and emboldened, people begin to throw stones at the criminals in the open cart. Frightened by the stoning, a horse bolts, and the cart tips over, killing one of the condemned men.

The story, based on events that actually transpired in the 1850s, is about what happens on the island during the next eight months—the time it takes for the guillotine (in French slang, a "widow") to arrive by ship from Paris. Neel Auguste, the remaining convicted killer (played by Emir Kusturica), is placed in the custody of the captain of the French military detachment (Daniel Auteuil) and the captain's compassionate wife, "Madame La" (Juliette Binoche). Though some of the authorities disapprove, Auguste is allowed a degree of freedom to help with gardening and repairs around town. Still rough around the edges, he nevertheless becomes a model citizen on his journey of penance. In one remarkable, selfless act, he helps save a life. Slowly, he wins the respect and genuine affection of the lonely people of the island.

The keepers of the law are faced with a dilemma—the prisoner has changed. Midway through the movie, a worried government official laments, "We condemned a criminal, and we'll execute a good person. Everyone here would like to have him for lunch on Sundays!"

The killer has changed, but so have the people of the island. Not one is willing to be the executioner. Even the Captain, once willing to do his part to uphold the law, refuses to allow his troops to aid in the beheading. The end of the story is as unforgiving as history itself, though the power of transformation has turned the world upside down. We are left to wonder who has truly won the day and what, in the end, has been lost.

A poster—issued jointly by Amnesty International, USA, and Death Penalty Focus—features pictures of eight children. One boy proudly wears his Boy Scout sash, displaying the numerous badges he has earned. Two faces—one black, the other white—sport infectious grins, sparkling eyes, dimples. One photo is of a naked toddler, soft, shy, and wrinkly. The boy in another photo has bags under his eyes. Another boy, smiling ear to ear, has freckles across his nose and is missing a front tooth. Only two boys look wary, on guard, as if they have already encountered too much that is unsettling, disturbing, traumatic.

Eight faces. No names. Underneath the photographs is the simple group identification: CURRENT DEATH ROW INMATES. At the top of the poster is one question: "Shouldn't We Be Asking What Went Wrong?" At the bottom is the statement: "We owe it to the innocent children they once were. Let's seek answers, not vengeance."

Looking at these photos, we are certain that something, somewhere went very wrong indeed, for these youngsters to end up on death row.

What happened? Here is evidence that there was a Before to the abhorrent After. In this Before of toothy grins and freckles, couldn't someone have intervened with help, if help was needed, or with encouragement and opportunity? What would it have taken to change the outcome for these boys—more funding for prenatal care? better schools? intervention into a violent home? a community playground? gun control? easy access to drug rehabilitation? literacy training? affordable housing? a sympathetic ear?

Cynics always laugh at such lists, as if these first-to-be-cut wish-list items were luxuries—as disposable as the people who need them. Under our current system, the Before gets short shrift, and children in need must almost fend for themselves, while the After is abundantly funded.

Prisons are our subsidized housing for the poor.

❖ *Today, virtually everyone in inner-city minority communities lives with knowledge of family in the prisons. Children often visit prisons to see loved ones more often than they have school field trips. Talk on the street is often about a kind of new age slavery, with predominantly black populations caged and housed in the prisons. Rappers from the worlds of contemporary hip-hop refer to the big prisons as the new slave galleons of our time.*
~ MARK LEWIS TAYLOR

Part of facing complexity is acknowledging that people can change. One way that they can change is by moving from innocent to troubled, and from troubled to twisted. Reading about the early lives of some people who wind up on death row is a lesson in lost opportunity, if not outright despair.

Our sympathies are naturally with the abused children. We loathe the cowards who slap them around or get them hooked on drugs, the ones who use children for sex or who sell their kids to the pornography industry. We weep for the little ones whose starved bodies and bruised faces occasionally make the headlines. We shake our heads and wonder—How can anyone do that to a child? We have no doubt that these are innocent victims.

They continue to win our sympathy until—Is it any surprise?—the day that they start to show the world what they have learned from their experiences. Then, it is as if they cross an unforgiving line in our hearts, moving lock, stock, and barrel from victim to violator, abused to abuser. They move from damaged to disposable and from sympathetic to scorned. For these people, there is no spectrum of tolerance, no middle ground of grace. Once over the line, they are not allowed back.

❖ *There are very few on death row who weren't abused. Take, for example, one of my clients from Florida. When he was six months old, his mother swapped him for a dining room table and it just went downhill from there. When he was three years old, they started sexually abusing him.*

~CLIVE STAFFORD-SMITH

For people on death row, the events of their lives are reduced to one act—the crime for which they have been condemned. It does not matter what came before—if they were decent sons or loving mothers or hard workers or dreamers of big dreams. It doesn't even matter if they once served their country in battle or ever saved a life, or if they committed untold selfless deeds. When a death sentence is read, time is frozen at the moment of the unforgiven crime.

On September 24, 1997, the state of Missouri intentionally killed Samuel McDonald. It did not matter that he had enlisted in the Army at age seventeen and served in Vietnam, where he had earned several medals for bravery. He killed a baby and an old woman, but that was in Vietnam, during the ordered "sweep" of a village. His participation, far from being considered criminal, was in the line of duty to his country, and the dead were deemed "collateral damage." Nevertheless, like other decorated Vietnam veterans, he turned to drugs, and his life entered a big downward spiral. In 1981, McDonald, high and suffering from post-traumatic stress disorder, shot and killed an off-duty police officer. His medals meant nothing. In the eyes of society, he was transformed from patriot to pariah.

Capital punishment is a system that cannot accommodate complexity. Those who support the death penalty deny the reality that people can change, and that there is potential for healing and growth.

Stephen Wayne Anderson survived a childhood of abuse and neglect with parents who were mentally disturbed and violent. In 1980, at the age of twenty-six, he shot and killed an eighty-one-year-old retired piano teacher, during a burglary gone wrong.

During his twenty years on death row, Anderson began to educate himself, (finally utilizing his 136 IQ), reading everything he could, even studying Latin. Worlds opened to him. He dreamed of libraries. He changed. He became a writer of novels, an off-Broadway play, numerous short stories, and thousands of poems. His writing was exceptional. He won several national awards, including the coveted first prize in a PEN (Poets, Essayists, and Novelists) contest. He was dubbed "a connoisseur of despair, the poet laureate of America's damned."

Though the daughters of the slain piano teacher argued against his execution, and though his court-appointed lawyer was deemed incompetent in several other trials, and though Anderson was a different person at age forty-eight from what he was the night he committed his crime, the state of California put him to death on January 29, 2002.

There is no room in capital punishment for people to change, except to go from living to dead.

Because Karla Faye Tucker was a woman with expressive brown eyes and a way with words, her life story caught media attention, and the world was made aware of several transformations in her life of thirty-eight years. One transformation came at the age of eight when her mother taught her the right way to roll a marijuana joint. When Karla was fourteen, her mother, a secretary by day and a call girl by night, turned Karla over to a room full of men, to be schooled in the art of adult sex, priming her for prostitution. Karla turned to heroin, dropped out of school, and began to run with a crowd that was at least as rough as her own mother.

Another transformation happened one night in June, 1983, when she and her boyfriend murdered two people with a hammer and a pickax. Both murderers were sentenced to death in the state of Texas, although the boyfriend died of liver disease before his execution date.

Another transformation occurred when Tucker was locked up. In the solitude of her cell, Tucker had time to contemplate her life and discover options she had never known. She earned her G.E.D. and took college courses until budget cuts ended the program. She immersed herself in Bible study and found solace, strength, and guidance in Scripture. She was given the opportunity to participate in several programs for troubled youth and began to dream of becoming, as she put it, "a positive contributor to our society."

Prisons are filled with people who have "found the Lord." It is easy to doubt the sincerity of such conversions, although it is a common experience of anyone in dire circumstances to suddenly call on the comfort and aid of Jesus and all the saints, Allah, Jehovah, Krishna, and the Buddha. But in Tucker's case, a wide variety of people, from prison personnel to old acquaintances, remarked on her dramatic and profound transformation. More than one observed that she had a certain glow of new life. Removed from her previous context, she seemed to wake up from a nightmare of drugs and violence to find new possibilities. Even the Houston detective J. C. Mosier, who originally arrested Tucker and saw the carnage at the crime scene, was persuaded that she was a "totally different person," and that her change of heart was genuine.

She sought forgiveness from the relatives of her victims, and her life was turned upside down when several, including Peggy Kurtz, the sister of the slain man, granted that forgiveness. In a lengthy letter to then-governor George W. Bush, Tucker wrote, "I know how this changed my life so completely that it is hard to recognize me in old pictures. I know that if this kind of love and forgiveness had the power to transform my life so completely for the good, it can be done in others."

In her letter to Governor Bush, Tucker outlined some of the ways she hoped she could use her life, if spared, for the good, arguing, "Fourteen-and-a-half years ago I was part of the problem. Now I am part of the solution. I come to you based on this, as an individual, asking you to please consider allowing me to continue on and reach out and help others keep from doing what I did. I am helping save lives now instead of taking lives and hurting others."

Though appeals for clemency on her behalf came from all corners of the globe—including from members of the United Nations, the World Council of Churches, the Pope, and TV evangelist Pat Robertson— Bush refused to grant a reprieve of any kind.

Karla Faye Tucker was strapped to a gurney on February 3, 1998, in Huntsville, Texas, making history as the first woman executed in that state since 1863. She used her last words to express the hope that her death would bring peace to the families of her victims. Then she said, "Warden Baggett, thank all of you so much. You have been so good to me. I love all of you very much. I will see you all when you get there. I will wait for you."

Outside of the prison, with hundreds of reporters and photographers, were anti-death penalty protesters. They were almost overwhelmed by a high-spirited pro-execution crowd. An estimated half of the latter were college students, who raucously sang, "Na na na na, na na na na, hey hey, good-bye." One man carried a sign, AXE AND YOU SHALL RECEIVE. TEXAS 2:1. Another sign read, FORGET INJECTION: USE A PICKAXE.

❖ *[The death penalty] denies the possibility of redemption and reform. No matter how great the sin, or how evil the crime, who are we to deny the possibility that through God's love, a human spirit might be redeemed, changed and transformed; that true regret and remorse might lead to repentance, atonement, even some healing; that the best qualities of humanity might be more fully realized? Who are we to deny such a possibility?*

~REPRESENTATIVE CLIFTON C. BELOW

Stanley "Tookie" Williams, once known as a cofounder of the deadly Crips street gang, is now known as the death row inmate nominated for a Nobel Prize. He has changed in his twenty years on death row. Daily, he rolls up his mattress to use as a desk in his nine-by-four-foot cell, where he writes books for children and youth, de-glamorizing the gang lifestyle and warning about the horrors of life in prison. He has also created the Internet Project for Street Peace, which links at-risk youths in the United States and abroad through E-mail and chat rooms.

He is now at the top of the list of those waiting to be executed in California.

What generally matters in the eyes of the State, once a verdict of guilt is reached, is the crime the condemned committed. That, and nothing more. Indeed, this narrow focus is precisely what allows us, as a society, to execute our own citizens.

❖ *Every inmate caught in this predicament spends a considerable amount of time on death row before being re-sentenced or killed. This time almost inevitably leads to change. The people who are being killed are not the people who are sentenced.*

~LOU JONES

In "The Model of the Thief," a short story by the late Alfred Gobell, an artist is commissioned to paint a large-scale crucifixion scene on three separate panels. The triptych is to depict Jesus on the cross and the two thieves who were crucified with him—the one thief, who mocked Jesus, and the other, who felt remorse.

To paint the portrait of the unrepentant thief, the artist needs a model. He goes to skid row to find someone with a bad attitude, someone callous, bored, and cynical. In the dark shadows, he comes upon a grubby man with a hardened face who is more than willing to be paid for sitting still. As the artist paints, the model talks about his life, and his talk is cocky, crude, and rude. The artist is glad when his work on the portrait of the unrepentant thief nears completion.

But, no sooner has he paid his model and thanked him, when the man insists that he can serve as the model for the repentant thief as well. He likes the money, the work is easy, and he is a good actor, able to conjure a look of remorse at will. Indeed, the artist has to agree that the crafty man is skilled at feigning shame, vulnerability and longing, and that the face he now presents is perfect for the image of the repentant thief. A new agreement is made between artist and model.

When the second painting is completed, the calculating model from skid row makes a half-hearted bid to pose for the third panel as well and serve as the model of Christ. He isn't surprised when the artist firmly rejects the proposal and shoos him out the door.

More than a year goes by and the artist paints the body of Jesus hanging on the cross but leaves the face blank since he needs a model and none has appeared.

One afternoon, as the discouraged artist stares with tired eyes at the incomplete work, a vision of Christ appears in the studio. "I have come to stand as a model," the pale vision says. The artist stares, in shock and then in alarm. This vision is not only flesh and blood, but it is his old model from skid row—transformed. For the sake of easy money, the man had sought to look like the Christ. In the process of fasting, consciously using solitude, and reading the Gospel story, his life has begun to heal and change. What was callous, has softened. What was wounded, has healed. The thief has become a true disciple.

As the story ends, the reader knows that the figures in the completed triptych will have the same face. On the first panel, the face will be hopeless and hardened; on the second, the face will be filled with longing and shame; on the third panel, the face will be of one who has looked into his heart and found the compassion of Jesus.

People can change. This is the complicated truth about life.

Varieties of Nonviolent Action
toward the Abolition
of Capital Punishment

📖 *Alice's Adventures in Wonderland* and
Through the Looking-Glass by Lewis Carroll

When little Alice falls through the rabbit hole, and later, when she steps into
the mirror, she finds herself in a topsy-turvy dream where almost nothing
makes sense. It is in this context that we meet the lively pack of cards, most
notably the Queen of Hearts, whose favorite command is "Off with her head!"

Alice thought she had never seen such a curious croquet-ground in
her life: it was all ridges and furrows; the croquet balls were live
hedgehogs, and the mallets live flamingoes, and the soldiers had to
double themselves up and stand on their hands and feet, to make
the arches . . . .

The players all played at once without waiting for turns, quar-
reling all the while, and fighting for the hedgehogs; and in a very
short time the Queen was in a furious passion, and went stamping
about, and shouting "Off with his head!" or "Off with her head!"
about once in a minute.

Alice began to feel very uneasy: to be sure, she had not as yet
had any dispute with the Queen, but she knew that it might happen
any minute, "and then," thought she, "what would become of me?
They're dreadfully fond of beheading people here: the great wonder is, that there's any one left alive!"

In 1973, *The Politics of Nonviolent Action*, a three-volume work by re-
searcher Gene Sharp, was published and immediately hailed as a land-

mark study of practical, tactical nonviolence. Sharp compiled historical examples of nonviolent action, identifying 198 specific tactics used in a variety of struggles around the globe. It is an inspiring list for anyone seeking creative ways to make social change because it includes everything from sit-ins to walk-outs, blockades to boycotts, protest disrobings to tax resistance.

Sharp wrote that people using nonviolent action apply something like jiujitsu. An opponent who is skilled at meeting violence with violence is thrown off balance by the surprise of nonviolent disobedience, noncooperation, or protest. There is strength in the unexpected, the unfamiliar. Another strength of nonviolence is that everyone who wishes to, can participate. Whereas violent tactics require that actions be taken primarily by those who are well-muscled, well-heeled, well-armed, or willing to risk arrest, nonviolent tactics can be employed by everyone including the young, the old, the fearful, the infirm, the couch potatoes, and the over-worked with mere minutes to spare.

❖ *The nonviolent movement, like any strong movement, must make room for those of us who aren't very brave. One of the values of nonviolence is that a person can be young or old, weak, sick, or frightened, and still find a way to fit in. This helps make it a democratic movement. It means it has room for me!*

~DAVID MCREYNOLDS

Another strength of nonviolent action is its ability to address complexity. Activist/writer Barbara Deming spoke often of the two hands of nonviolence. With one hand, the nonviolent activist says "Stop the wrong you are doing!" With this hand we refuse to cooperate, we refuse to pay, we disrupt business as usual.

But the nonviolent activist then uses the other hand, out-stretched, to indicate connection. With this hand we say, "I won't cast you out of the human race. I have faith that you can make a better choice than you are making now, and I'll be here when you do. We are a part of one another."

This ability to address complexity, to keep open the possibility of societal and personal change, and to make sure the means we use are not contradictory to the end we have in mind—this is the strength of nonviolent action.

❖ . . . *if the complicated truth is that many of the oppressed are also oppressors and many of the oppressors are also oppressed, nonviolent confrontation is the only form of confrontation that allows us to respond realistically to such complexity. In this kind of struggle we address ourselves always both to that which we refuse to accept from others and to that which we can respect in them, have in common with them—however much or little that may be.*

~BARBARA DEMING

For the purposes of this chapter, I have compiled examples and anecdotes of nonviolent action taken to abolish capital punishment. Using Sharp's three basic categories of nonviolent action, the examples are divided into "protest and persuasion"—actions with which we identify the problem, educate, and inform; "noncooperation"—actions with which we demonstrate our refusal to participate in the wrong we have named; and "intervention"—actions designed to throw a monkey wrench into the works.

What follows are stories of actions taken by people who have found creative and nonviolent ways to "defy death" in their work to abolish capital punishment and to dismantle the execution machinery of the United States criminal justice system. It is my hope that the actions described in this chapter will inspire our collective imaginations. We learn from each other; spin, spark, and reshape ideas gleaned from another's creative action; borrow from the tested and true to fashion something new. May each story spawn a myriad more until we have rid our country of the "ultimate punishment."

I. NONVIOLENT PROTEST AND PERSUASION

❖ *We must show the executioner's hands each time and force everyone to look at them . . . otherwise society admits it kills without knowing what it is saying or doing.*

~ALBERT CAMUS

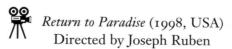 *Return to Paradise* (1998, USA)
Directed by Joseph Ruben

In a vast, grim Malaysian prison, one American inmate, imprisoned on drug possession charges, hears another being dragged through the hallways and into the courtyard to the scaffold. He stretches to grasp the bars of the tiny window in his cell. Pulling himself up, he sees, in the bleak morning light, his friend struggle and cry as the noose is put around his neck. From the confines of his cell, the witness shouts out, "I see you. You are not alone. I see you." He yells this over and over. "I see you. I see you."

Actions that Make Us Look and Look Again

Banner Projects

The congregation of the Church of Gethsemane, a Presbyterian church in Brooklyn, has made it a priority to fight societal complacency toward capital punishment. Whenever someone in the United States is executed, this church hangs a 78 inch by 52 inch banner outside its second-story window, witnessing in big block letters: ONE MORE PERSON WAS EXECUTED TODAY.

The banner project was conceived as part of a Capital Punishment Awareness Campaign in 1994. The founding pastor of Gethsemane, the Reverend Dr. Constance M. Baugh, got the idea when she read about the NAACP's anti-lynching campaign in the early 20th century. Each time news was received that a person had been lynched, the NAACP hung a banner outside its New York office that read, A MAN WAS LYNCHED YESTERDAY. It is estimated that between 1882 and 1925, over 3,700 lynchings took place in the United States, but these atrocities were largely ignored or minimized in the mainstream press. The NAACP attempted to keep the shame of lynching in the public eye, or at least in the eyes of the passersby.

So too, the Church of Gethsemane fights the current trend to make executions routine, non-newsworthy, invisible. Its banner is a shout to all who see it, "Look at what is being done in your name! A life is being taken today! Be aware! Care!"

Bells and Drapes

In Medford, Massachusetts, Dorothy Briggs, a Catholic nun, has promoted an idea similar to Gethsemane's banner project. She calls it For Whom the Bells Toll. Churches across the country are invited to toll their bells for two minutes at 6 P.M. on the day of an execution in the United States or, when bells are not available, cover their doors with a dramatic black drape of mourning. In their Sunday bulletins, participat-

Banner action at the Church of Gethsemane. Photo by Joyce Pyle

ing churches are asked to include an explanation of the project and its goal of keeping people mindful of the death penalty.

One participating church is St. Ignatius of Antioch Episcopal Church on Manhattan's Upper West Side. Father H. Gaylord Hitchcock, Jr., the church's rector, told a *New York Times* reporter, "It's often quite a lonely witness. . . . I've had messages on my voicemail, saying we were un-Christians." Lonely or not, Reverend Hitchcock and his parishioners are faithful. On a day when someone in the United States is being executed, they toll the church's old iron bell, once for every year in the life of the person being put to death. If more than one execution is scheduled, they toll the bell a symbolic thirty-three times to represent Jesus's age at the time of his death on the cross. On the sidewalk in front of the church, the witnesses distribute fliers listing the names of both the condemned and their victims, then read from the *Book of Common Prayer*.

Street Theater

On evenings when an execution is scheduled somewhere in the nation, members of The Living Theatre gather at Times Square in New York City to perform *Not in My Name*, a protest play against the death penalty.

The Living Theatre was founded in 1947 by Julian Beck and Judith Malina and has maintained a firm commitment to social and political change through radical theater, with ideals laid down by Antonin Artaud who called for "a theater where the actors are like victims burning at the stake, signaling through the flames." It combines ritual, spectacle, and political confrontation.

Not in My Name is a play that includes elements of song, Greek tragedy, and Artaud's Theatre of Cruelty, and involves actors, singers, activists, and death penalty abolitionists who have attended a workshop to learn how to perform the piece.

At the time of the performance, a playbill is passed out to onlookers. The cover art is Escher-esque, depicting a circle of six hollering bald

The playbill-cover art for *Not in My Name*. Artist: Luba Lukova

men. Five of the men are stabbing each other in the back. The sixth has broken the cycle and is reaching both hands up and out of the circle of violence and revenge.

Colosseum Campaign

The Colosseum in Rome, completed in 80 C.E., was once famous as the amphitheater where 45,000 cheering and jeering spectators could watch gladiators fight slaves, prisoners, each other, and wild beasts to the death. Today it has become the international symbol of opposition to the death penalty. It is flooded with golden light whenever a country abolishes the death penalty or a death row inmate's sentence is commuted. The sponsors of the Colosseum campaign include the United Nations, Amnesty International, Hands Off Cain, the city of Rome, the Vatican, and the Community of Sant' Egidio.

Death Row Execution-Day Protest

When Ziyon Yisrayah (Tommy Smith) was executed by lethal injection in Indiana in 1996, inmates throughout the penitentiary drummed on their cell-bars and walls. One prisoner, Sadiki, documented the protest and found significance in the thunderstorm that broke during the execution. He later E-mailed his thoughts to Princeton theology professor Mark Lewis Taylor who included the following paragraphs in the book *The Executed God*,

> As We grieved de best way We knew how, de whole earth seemed to shake. Soon you could not tell de difference between our grief and de universe's: Her pain was our pain; Her rain and our tears were inseparable. We had all become one-verse (uni-verse).
>
> I recall wondering as I kicked and shook de bars, if Ziyon could hear or feel us. Diz made me put all my energy into it, b'cuz I wanted him to hear and feel us, in spite of distance between Us and de murder room. . . . It was as if We were trying to send a message out to Ziyon and We were all writing with de same pen. De message read: "We luv you Bro, and We will continue to struggle for liberation."

The Waiting Room—*Art Installation*

When he was a young man, Richard Kamler overheard an accomplished artist say, "Through art, we can change the laws of the world."

Inspired by this, Kamler has since used art to address the world he first encountered when he signed up to work with prisoners in San Quentin.

"It was the din that hit me—people in your face shouting, the TV blaring, metal on metal, concrete on concrete." Prison sounds made their way into Kamler's multimedia, interactive art installation called *The Waiting Room*.

In this re-creation of the San Quentin waiting room, visitors hear the ticking of a giant metronome, with a pendulum of blue light relentlessly marking the time. There is also the sound of an amplified heartbeat that occasionally pauses. It is the silence that startles.

As visitors move through the installation, they are invited to take a meal tray from the "Last Suppers" exhibit. Each is dull gray, with a name and execution date, last words, and lead sculpted into the shape of food the condemned requested for their last meal—a burger and fries, an apple. Some trays are empty.

Stones—*Death Penalty Art Show*

Marylyn Felion, an artist and activist, was a witness to the execution of Robert Williams on December 2, 1997, in Nebraska. She had been corresponding with him for some time and promised to help him take that last walk. Even before she met him in person, she began using his impending execution as a theme in her paintings. She called the series *Stones*, remembering what Jesus said to the crowd of men intent on stoning to death a woman accused of adultery, "Let the one among you who is without sin cast the first stone."

Felion's portrait of Robert Williams has been seen around the country as part of the touring-art exhibit that resulted from the *National Catholic Reporter's* search for images of Christ in the new millennium. It is entitled *Christ as a Poor, Black, Death Row Inmate*.

T-Shirt Action

Death penalty abolitionists at Eastern Mennonite University in Harrisonburg, Virginia raised enough money to buy T-shirts bearing anti-death penalty slogans in bulk, which are then given free to students and faculty on campus.

When an execution is scheduled in Virginia, people with the free T-shirts wear them for the day. "It really makes an impact on campus when everywhere you go you see people wearing the message, especially when you count the teachers," one activist said. Popular slogans on T-shirts and baseball caps, buttons and bumper stickers (available from Abolition Wear) include STOP EXECUTIONS NOW, I OPPOSE THE DEATH PENALTY: DON'T KILL FOR ME, WHY DO WE KILL PEOPLE WHO KILL PEOPLE TO SHOW THAT KILLING PEOPLE IS WRONG?, and AN EYE FOR AN EYE MAKES THE WHOLE WORLD BLIND.

Symbolic Sound Action
On September 25, 1999, over fifty people set up ladders in various traffic islands throughout Philadelphia. Perched on top, they held up signs encouraging passing drivers to HONK FOR MUMIA while fellow activists passed out leaflets as a part of the effort to educate and agitate on behalf of celebrated death row inmate Mumia Abu-Jamal.

Mock Executions
Chapel Hill activists have staged mock executions on the campus of the University of North Carolina. Students stop to watch between classes as the group acts out, step by step, the dry, disengaged, methodical routine of putting someone to death.

❖ *Never doubt that a small group of thoughtful, committed citizens can change the world. Indeed, it is the only thing that ever has.*

~MARGARET MEAD

Actions that Educate

Leafleting

Philadelphia—Publishing and distributing fliers is a common method of educating the public used by groups advocating social change. On October 19, 1999, members of the Pennsylvania Abolitionists United Against the Death Penalty (PA Abolitionists) had planned to lead a teach-in outside the Criminal Justice Center in Philadelphia. When they arrived at 8:30 that morning, they found fifty police officers, sheriff's deputies, and street barricades. The sheriff's office had declared the area a "no-protest zone."

Seven PA Abolitionists tried to pass out a brochure—Equal Justice USA's "How Racism Riddles the U.S. Death Penalty," but were arrested within two minutes. The police harassed someone videotaping the event, a woman who was simply holding the fliers, and supportive bystanders. A man wearing a sweatshirt proclaiming, I OPPOSE THE DEATH PENALTY: DON'T KILL FOR ME was told he could be arrested if he wore the shirt within two blocks of the Criminal Justice Center. The arrested, who became known as the Abolitionist Seven, were charged with "obstructing the application of justice through picketing" and were held for 26 hours.

San Francisco—That same day, one thousand people marched through the streets of San Francisco protesting the pending execution of Mumia Abu-Jamal. They marched from downtown to a shopping center, where they chanted "Tear down prisons / Wall by wall. / We're gonna free / Mumia Abu-Jamal!" Several of the demonstrators then took an escalator to the upper level, leaned over the balcony and dropped informational fliers on the shoppers below.

Marches

Brooklyn—The March of 100 Black Men took place on January 31, 1999, in downtown Brooklyn. The one hundred men, dressed in black, stood in two silent, straight-backed lines. Suddenly, they broke into a Call and Response:

LEADER:	Who are we?
MEN:	Black men!
LEADER:	What we gonna do?
MEN:	Free Mumia Abu-Jamal
LEADER:	How we gonna do it?
MEN:	Brick by brick and wall by wall,
	We're gonna free Mumia Abu-Jamal.
LEADER:	If Mumia dies?
MEN:	Fire in the skies!

At that, the men silently turned and marched four miles through the streets of Brooklyn, stopping in parks and shopping centers with their message. The march ended at the notorious seventy-seventh police precinct, which had been plagued by charges of corruption. One of the organizers, a member of the New Afrikan Liberation Front, said,

"Today's march was more effective in reaching and educating our people than fifteen conferences, ten community meetings, and five leadership meetings."

Manhattan—Shouting "Mumia is fearless / So are we. / We won't stop / Until he's free"—high school and college students staged a Stop the Execution of Mumia Abu-Jamal Speak Out at New York City's Columbus Circle on September 21, 1999. Then, they marched down Broadway to Times Square, distributing informational fliers as they went.

Madison, Wisconsin—On September 25, 1999, following a week of teach-ins, films, forums, dances and art shows throughout Wisconsin, over two hundred protesters rallied at the state capitol in Madison to demand a new trial for Abu-Jamal. After listening to speeches, they marched through the streets, stopping first to picket at the new Dane County Jail where prisoners could be seen waving from the windows, and then proceeded to a wrap-up rally at a local police station.

Montréal—That same day, in Montréal, three hundred anti-death penalty activists, acting in solidarity with their United States counterparts, marched through downtown to Planet Hollywood, a restaurant and boutique which, according to march organizers, sells expensive clothing made by prisoners in Oregon who are forced to work for less than $1.80 an hour. In preparing for the action, death penalty abolitionists had distributed 13,000 fliers and put up 1,200 posters.

Walks

New Orleans-to-Baton Rouge Walk—*Dead Man Walking*, published in 1993, is a book by Sister Helen Prejean about her experiences as a spiritual adviser to death row inmates. Her stories have captured the imaginations of millions and galvanized a movement of people seeking to abolish capital punishment. In the book, she wrote of her participation in an October, 1984, New Orleans-to-Baton Rouge Walk. Forty people made the eighty mile trek to kick off a statewide information campaign about the death penalty in Louisiana. She wrote,

It's my first time meeting people in the media. I notice how friendly many of them are. After the interviews I always shake hands and thank them for coming out, the reporters and the camera people too; and before the walk is over I have quite a collection of their personal cards, which I file so I can call on them in the future. Reflecting back after ten years, I realize now, even more than I did then, just how crucial the media are to public education on this issue, and I am struck by how many reporters and journalists become sympathetic to the cause of abolition once they become knowledgeable about the issue.

We walk in the sunshine. . . . We'll do twenty-five miles each day. When people drop behind the crowd (people such as me, with short legs), a van picks us up and brings us to the front. That way we keep a brisk pace. Everybody's full of chatter. Some sing. One young fellow plays a kazoo. . . .

Many people, barreling along the highway, energetically signal their response to our cause: they put thumbs down; they flip us the middle finger; they shout "Fry the bastards"; they call us "bleeding-heart liberals"; they call us "commies." But every now and then we hear a horn and see a thumb up, and we all wave and cheer.

Children's Crusade to Death Row—This three-day, thirty-mile walk was organized by fifth-through-ninth graders from the Bruderhof community in Farmington, Pennsylvania, in August 1997. The members of Bruderhof religious communities are pacifists who share everything in common, as the early Christians did, and are active leaders in the fight against the death penalty.

Close to five hundred people—children accompanied by teachers, parents, and adult activists—participated in the march from the Bruderhof community to the SCI-Green, in Waynesburg, Pennsylvania. This Supermax (super-maximum security) state prison houses over half the state's death row inmates, including, at that time, Mumia Abu-Jamal.

On the first day, the crusaders set off in the rain and walked fifteen miles. That night they set up camp in a field, enjoyed a barbecue and a concert of rap and dancing. They read aloud an endorsement from Rage Against the Machine, a popular band, to the delight of the young people.

The next day they walked eight miles. When they stopped to set up camp for the night, they posed in a field, forming the word LIFE in giant letters for the news helicopter flying overhead. The children were pleased that the local media covered their event, as did CNN and *USA Today*. The second evening was a night of singing and emotional speeches.

It rained again the third and final day of the walk, but this did not dampen the children's spirits. They sang, waved their signs, and danced the last stretch to the prison. There, they were met by prison guards. The children gave the guards flowers and then released colorful balloons into the sky that bore the words ABOLISH THE DEATH PENALTY.

A number of endorsers sent messages of encouragement to the children, including death row inmate Mumia Abu-Jamal whose grandson was one of the marchers. Folksinger Pete Seeger also sent a message, as did Ramsey Clark, the former attorney general of the United States, who said, "I hope that everyone who sees the children march for justice, against the death penalty, will take the message to heart so that they may live and love each other."

Bicycle Tour
Trek 2001 was a father-and-son bicycle tour taken in the summer of 2001 to spread an anti-death penalty message following the June 11 execution of Timothy McVeigh. According to James Colver, a 22-year-old sophomore at Trinity Lutheran College in the state of Washington, "My mission this summer is mainly to help educate those I meet about the message of peace and reconciliation through Jesus explained in the gospel. I will encourage everyone to look at Jesus for the answer to criminals, and not resort to capital punishment as a false means of justice." James and his father Robert biked from Bar Harbor, Maine, to Fort Myers, Florida, with their message of love and reconciliation.

Motorcades
In September, 1999, the Northern Maryland Anti-Racist Action organized a seven-car caravan. Each car carried passengers who used a loudspeaker to tell the story of death row inmate Mumia Abu-Jamal as they drove through the streets of Baltimore. The cars stopped at various busy locations where the participants could leaflet and answer questions.

Pilgrimages
For ten days in April, 2002, people participating in the New York Interfaith Prison Pilgrimage traveled by van to more than a dozen prisons

dotting the state. As they approached each "correctional facility" they walked, passing out informative brochures and inviting local residents to join them "for an hour, a day or more" or for lunch, a rally, or an evening forum.

The purpose of the walk was to raise awareness of the current criminal justice system and to call for the creation of a new system that would embody the principles of restorative justice. Along the way, the participants engaged in open dialogue about our society's reliance on prisons and urged more cost-effective solutions that have the potential to restore victims and offenders. They spoke of reconciliation over retribution.

The pilgrimage was a joint project of the Judicial Process Commission of Rochester and the Prison Action Connection of Western New York Peace Center, headquartered in nearby Buffalo. Local churches and community groups provided meals and overnight accommodations for the pilgrims. People and organizations across the state were invited to endorse the pilgrimage, provide goods and/or services, or make a financial donation. This action became both a networking tool and an educational event.

Speaking Tours and Storytelling

Journey of Hope—From Violence to Healing is a project led by murder-victim family members. Since 1993, the Journey storytellers have toured the country, educating the public by telling of their tragedies and their struggles to heal, and by opening dialogue on the death penalty and its alternatives. They have visited schools, colleges, churches, and other venues, telling why they have sought compassionate action instead of revenge for the murder of their loved ones.

Bill Pelke, a cofounder of Journey of Hope, has served as its president. In 1985, in Gary, Indiana, his beloved 78-year-old grandmother, Ruth, opened her door to four ninth-grade girls. Thinking they had come to her for Bible lessons, she invited them inside. Within minutes, she was stabbed a total of thirty-three times while her house was ransacked. The girls found ten dollars.

Paula Cooper, only fifteen at the time of the crime, was sentenced to death, becoming the youngest female on death row in America. Through a long process of transformation, Bill Pelke, who originally supported the execution of Cooper, had a change of heart. He began visiting the troubled teen and realized that his grandmother would never want this young woman put to death in her name. Pelke successfully worked to overturn her sentence.

After retiring from thirty years service with Bethlehem Steel, Pelke pledged to continue his work to end the death penalty in America. He purchased a tour bus so that he and others with Journey of Hope can travel across the country with their powerful witness.

Voices for a New Justice Tour—In March, 2003, New Yorkers Against the Death Penalty (NYADP) sponsored a speaking tour of four unlikely allies—two victims of violent crime and two family members of those who committed violent crimes. Gary Wright, a victim of the "Unabomber" Ted Kaczynski, was on the panel along with the Unabomber's brother, death penalty abolitionist David Kaczynski. Bill Babbitt, whose brother Manny had been executed for murder, was a featured speaker on the tour, as was Bud Welch, whose daughter was killed in the 1995 Oklahoma City bombing. They brought their stories to high school, college, and church audiences throughout New York State, and told about their efforts to understand and forgive the troubled people who had so affected their lives. Together Bud, Gary, David, and Bill spoke out against revenge-oriented capital punishment and in favor of a system of restorative justice.

Dead Man Walking—Sister Helen Prejean tries to spend fifteen days each month on the road, telling stories about the people she's met on death row, and inviting her listeners to think carefully about capital punishment. "We rely on the power of the story to influence people and make them think. It's how Jesus sent out his message—through parables."

Prejean believes in storytelling. She says, "To reach out to people, you have to tell stories. This is one of the reasons I think *Dead Man Walking* in all its forms touched so many people, because in my stories I allowed people to see how it was for me, and for the inmate, and for the families involved."

Dead Man Walking was made into a movie directed by Tim Robbins and starring Susan Sarandon and Sean Penn. Prejean says,

In nearly twenty years of traveling around the country on speaking tours, I have realized that the American people are ready to talk about the death penalty. They need someone to take them through the discussion. The book . . . was my first opportunity to do this. I was pleased when the film was made . . . because I knew we were going to have a new, tangible way to help the American people reflect on the death penalty.

The movie became an educational tool in several communities. The American Civil Liberties Union (ACLU) advocated arranging for pre- or post-movie discussions of the death penalty at libraries or restaurants near theaters where the movie was being shown. The ACLU also suggested distributing informative brochures before and after the movie or setting up a literature table nearby. They urged commenting on the film in Internet chat room conversations. Community or church groups could also rent the video and arrange for a movie-and-discussion event.

Bob Gross is the author of *The Death Penalty: A Guide for Christians* and has served as Executive Director of the National Coalition to Abolish the Death Penalty. He wrote a "Discussion Guide for the Film/Video *Dead Man Walking*," designed for use in Christian and Jewish communities, as a way to assist groups in considering the issues raised by the movie. Gross suggested several formats for using the "Guide," recommended beginning with time for "initial reactions and feelings," and outlined a range of discusson questions (e.g., "What do you think of Helen's attempt to minister with 'both sides'—with the murderer and with the families of the murder victims?" "How does Ezekiel 33:11 apply to the question of capital punishment? 'As I live, says the Lord God, I have no pleasure in the death of the wicked, but that the wicked turn from their ways and live.'" and "Were your beliefs regarding capital punishment changed by watching this film? If so, how?").

Another way of telling Sister Prejean's story came in the form of an opera, also entitled *Dead Man Walking*, with music by Jake Heggie and libretto by Terrence McNally. Both the film and the opera focus on Prejean's personal transformation, as she moves into the bleak and harsh world of death row. We see her stumble, in confusion, unsure of herself and her purpose, struggling with misgivings about befriending a convicted killer, unsure of what to say to the bewildering young man about to be executed. It is precisely the story of her growing confidence and sense of purpose that empowers by example. She stumbles like I do, we think. She's afraid, just like I am. She's unsure too. We identify and see ourselves with the potential to grow, as she has grown.

About the experience of seeing the opera, Helen Prejean has written:

> True art brings you to both sides of a conflict. Through *Dead Man Walking*, I see audience members going to a deeper place within themselves. We see a murder, and then we see an execution. Are they essentially the same thing, or are they different? Is that the only way to respond as a society, or are there alternatives? The opera shows us we can look at different options in regards to using the death penalty. Art helps us explore alternatives, allows us to make new choices, and brings us to a deeper place where all this reflection can happen. This opera is particularly helpful as audiences navigate the moral dilemmas that surround capital punishment. . . .
>
> I am amazed when I look back over the last two decades at how the discussion on the death penalty has grown and matured, but yet we are still finding innocent people on death row. It is going to take the books and the movies and the news programs and of course the operas to continue this discussion, and to keep the American public moving forward in their awareness and their advocacy.

Public Hearings

Philadelphia—In March, 1996, three days of public hearings on the death penalty were held at City Hall in the "City of Brotherly Love." The hearings were set-up and sponsored by the National Commission on Capital Punishment, formed by the Bruderhof Foundation and the James E. Chaney Foundation (named for the civil rights worker slain in 1964). A wide variety of witnesses and experts spoke at the hearings, including a man freed from death row by DNA testing, a mother of a murder victim, several mothers of death row prisoners, and scholars, community activists, and clergy. The testimonies were later compiled and sent to members of Congress, the White House, and the Justice Department and were made available for use in schools, universities, and by interested individuals.

New York City—On January 22, 2001, a news conference and public hearing was attended by about one hundred people who joined to urge the New York City Council to pass a resolution supporting a moratorium on the death penalty. Speakers included exonerated former death row inmates, murder victims' family members, legal experts like Barry Scheck of The Innocence Project, and various religious leaders.

Teaching in the Classroom

Deborah Cordonnier, an adjunct faculty member at Rider University in New Jersey, makes it a point to assign a death penalty project in her classes. Whether it is a class in "Research Writing" or "Experiencing Race, Class, and Gender in the U.S." she introduces the topic. "The students never know my position," she says. The point of the assignment is to enable the students to look carefully at and think deeply about the issue of capital punishment and then let them draw their own conclusions. To assist them, Cordonnier invites guest speakers into the classroom—authors, attorneys, parents of murdered children, activists.

Although she does not impose her point of view, Cordonnier has noticed that, when students do the research and learn the facts about capital punishment, usually three or four students out of twenty change from being for the death penalty to against it. "Those three or four add up, when you consider I have been teaching in various venues since 1982."

Presentation of Awards

Occasions on which awards are given for anti-death penalty work can also be opportunities to educate and inform.

Abolitionist of the Year—On October 3, 1998, Father Patrick Delahanty was given the Abolitionist of the Year award by the National Coalition to Abolish the Death Penalty during the organization's annual conference. The priest had worked diligently in support of legislation to ban executions of mentally retarded people and to remove racial bias from Kentucky's capital sentencing process. Father Delahanty used his acceptance speech to encourage others to take a strong stand and not give in to apathy or defeat, saying:

> The British didn't think that Mahatma Gandhi would ever kick them out of India. And they were certainly mistaken. Others didn't think that Martin Luther King and many of the people that we honor over and over would ever be successful. And they were suc-

cessful. We have begun, and we continue, to be engaged in that struggle.

Everybody in this room is important in this struggle. It's sad to hear people say that some people feel they don't have any power or authority. Please, please communicate that they do have power and authority, and what they need to do is make their voices known and they will achieve the same kinds of victories that we have seen happening in Kentucky and in other places.

Thurgood Marshall Journalist Award—Naming an award after a leader in the death penalty abolitionist movement can make us mindful that we are part of a long-term effort. The Death Penalty Information Center established the Thurgood Marshall Journalist Award in 1996, to recognize writers and producers who have made an exceptional contribution to the understanding of the problems associated with capital punishment. The purpose of the award is to encourage investigation by journalists into the way the death penalty is actually applied in the United States. Thurgood Marshall, an African American, was a Supreme Court Justice who opposed capital punishment.

Awards could be named after other abolitionists like the Italian author of *On Crimes and Punishments*, Cesare Beccaria (1738–94). He argued against the retributive approach to punishment, which tends to be retaliatory and vengeance-oriented. Instead, he promoted punishment which stressed reform and served to prevent further crime.

Another early reformer was Dr. Benjamin Rush (1746–1813), a signer of the Declaration of Independence. He wrote an important paper against public punishments, which he read at Benjamin Franklin's home on March 9, 1787. He went on to begin a campaign to abolish the death penalty in America.

It is good to name and honor people who inspire us. As we tell their stories, we enable each other to learn from their examples.

❖ *I feel . . . blessed to be with such brave and prophetic people who must feel like the prophets of old—crying in the wilderness. I gain strength from people like Sister Chris Mulready who is tough and focused and unflappable and unstoppable. Her energy gives me energy. She is truly one of God's great warriors.*

I also gain strength from the JusticeWorks Community in Park Slope, Brooklyn at Gethsemane Presbyterian Church and from the Rev-

erend Connie Baugh who works so hard and so creatively against capital punishment.

~REVEREND DAVID DYSON

Actions that Influence

Letter-writing Campaigns

Urgent Action Network—In 1998, the Amnesty International (AI) chapter at Centerville High School in Centerville, Ohio, successfully involved 175 students in an Urgent Action writing workshop and follow-up letter-writing actions.

The students visited classrooms to talk about Amnesty International USA and the "Urgent Action Network." They put announcements over the school public-address system and passed out fliers to publicize a letter-writing workshop. At each subsequent monthly meeting, after reading aloud messages received from prisoners of conscience, they set aside the last twenty minutes for letter-writing. The group used proceeds from its fund-raising events to pay for the postage.

AI's Urgent Action Network offers an organized program of letter-writing, providing a guide to participation, background information about the various appeals, addresses, and sample messages.

AI's list of "Basic Tips for Writing Appeals to Government Officials" includes the following advice, useful for anyone writing a letter of persuasion:

(1) Familiarize yourself with the specific list of concerns.
(2) Be brief.
(3) Be factual. Do not discuss ideology or politics.
(4) Be polite. Assume the official is not informed but is willing to seek a remedy to the human rights violation.
(5) Show respect.
(6) Be unequivocal in the expression of your concern for the imprisoned person.
(7) Write in English.
(8) Write clearly. Make it plain and legible.
(9) Use shortcuts to make your letter-writing as easy as possible. For example, certain paragraphs may be copied into a variety of files and edited as needed.

Not in *My* Name—Several days before the June 11, 2001, execution of Timothy McVeigh, the Kansas Coalition Against the Death Penalty (KsCADP) Board issued a statement under the title, "Not in *Our* Name." Acknowledging that McVeigh's actions in Oklahoma City caused immeasurable pain and suffering, the Board questioned the notion that the State had to make the same choice McVeigh had made—killing and death. The statement concluded,

> When we snuff out McVeigh's life, we will have engaged in a show of brute force in response to the incredible violence he used. We will be sending the message that the answer to our problems is more killing. We will memorialize the Oklahoma City victims by creating another grieving family . . . Executions continue the cycle of violence and foster revenge and retaliation. Alternatives exist to protect society from Timothy McVeigh. So, when he goes to the death chamber, let one thing be clear: Not in *Our* Name!

KsCADP had launched the "Not in *My* Name" project in the fall of 1999 as a letter-writing campaign to abolish the death penalty. Noting that "Silence is equated with support," the activist organization urged all concerned people to copy prepared letters from the group's Web site, add their names and mail them to KsCADP or simply E-mail their signatures. According to the project description, "The Not in *My* Name letters will be shared with Kansas decision makers so that they are more fully informed about how Kansans feel on this issue."

> ❖ *The seeds for the total abolition of the death penalty are already in the ground. We don't have to change public opinion as much as we have to educate and coalesce groups that we already know will join the fight. We need to make it more and more respectable for death penalty abolitionists to come out of the closets. . . . If we keep our eye on that prize, and remember that history is on our side and step back occasionally to see the tremendous progress that we are making, the fight against the death penalty will eventually end in victory.*
>
> ~MICHAEL L. RADELET

Petition Drives

In January, 2000, in Illinois, then-Governor George Ryan imposed a moratorium on executions in his state, after thirteen death row inmates were exonerated there. Since that time, calls for a moratorium on the death penalty have come from all parts of the country. This impetus has spawned a nationwide Moratorium Campaign, the primary focus of which is the collection of signatures for use in lobbying state and federal legislators to suspend executions.

United Nations—In December, 2000, Sister Helen Prejean led a delegation of activists to the United Nations to present a petition calling for a worldwide moratorium on the death penalty. The petition was presented to UN Secretary General Kofi Annan. In her "Report from the Front" that month, Sister Prejean described the day:

> On December 18 we presented 3.2 million moratorium signatures to Kofi Annan at the U.N. What a princely man. . . . He walked in and there was a quiet, powerful energy in the room. He breathes integrity. He shook our hands, received the signatures, took photos with us and said simply that frail and fallible state governments can't be trusted to kill their citizens, that mistakes are made and once a person is killed, the mistake can't be corrected. Simple. Direct. And you knew he meant every word he said. I promised him we'd be back next year with 10 million signatures, and he said, "you'll be working hard." Which we will. Every soul reading this, know that we have a web page where you can sign on line for a moratorium on the death penalty. . . . Please visit our site and sign on and give the E-mail addresses of friends who will then get a letter saying you've signed on and are inviting them, too.

Syracuse, New York—At a Moratorium 2000 event in Syracuse, New York, members of People Against the Death Penalty of Central New York held a news conference and honored Michael Wilson, a high school student, who had collected more than five hundred signatures for the Moratorium 2000 Petition. Three local churches rang their bells at noon in a publicized effort of support for the Moratorium. Activists also used the occasion to present the Syracuse City Council and Onondaga County Legislature with requests to pass a death penalty moratorium resolution.

Stop Killing Kids Campaign—The National Coalition to Abolish the Death Penalty (NCADP) launched their "Stop Killing Kids Campaign" in the spring of 1998 with a national press conference. Charging that the United States policy of sentencing children to death is a national failure, the group quoted a statement from the Supreme Court, "Youth crime as such is not the offender's fault; offenses by the young also represent a failure of family, school, and the social system, which share responsibility for the development of America's youth."

The group further cited racial discrimination, noting that African Americans make up a large majority of juvenile offenders who are executed, and claimed that the United States is the "world-leader" in sentencing children to death, keeping questionable company at the present time with Iran, Pakistan, Yemen, Saudi Arabia, and Nigeria.

A centerpiece of the "Stop Killing Kids Campaign" was a student-led petition drive. Admonishing the youth population, "Don't let the government continue to murder your peers," NCADP issued suggestions for ways students could be organized, creative, and energetic in collecting signatures.

❖ *Just by living our lives, consuming space and resources, we are making a difference. Our choice is what kind of difference to make.*
~FRAN PEAVEY

Date-specific Actions

Birthday Action—"Millions for Mumia," part of the global campaign to stop the execution of Mumia Abu-Jamal, included a celebration of the inmate's forty-fifth birthday. On April 24, 1999, twenty thousand demonstrators marched, danced, chanted, and sang their way through the streets of Philadelphia and plastered the downtown area with stickers calling for Mumia's release.

Christmas Action—On December 25, 1998, members of an anti-death penalty group marched to Rome's St. Peter's Square from the Campo dei Fiori. This was where Giordano Bruno, an Italian monk, had become a martyr to science, burned at the stake in 1600 for the heresy of defending the Copernican hypothesis that the earth was *not* the center of the universe. The marchers were greeted at the Square by Pope John Paul II who had just delivered the traditional *Urbi et Orbi* (to the city and the world) message, this time including in it an urgent call to end capital punishment.

Juneteenth Action—Juneteenth, observed every June 19, commemorates the day, in 1865, when African slaves in Texas finally learned that they had been legally free since January 1, 1863. Uninformed of their freedom, the Africans had been tricked into continued captivity for two and a half years.

In 2002, the Texas Death Penalty Abolition Movement (TDPAM) used Juneteenth as a day to call attention to the plight of death row inmates at the Polunsky Unit, a maximum security "isolation" prison in Livingston. The demonstrators also used the occasion to educate the public about a significant loophole in the United States Constitution: the Thirteenth Amendment, which makes slavery illegal, includes the phrase, "except as punishment for a crime." According to TDPAM, this clause allowed savvy slave owners to move their plantations from the private to the public sector.

Like the Birthday, Christmas, and Juneteenth actions, other dates can serve as a focusing tool for an anti-death penalty agenda. The following calendar dates may spark an idea for action:

⤙ A CALENDAR OF ACTION OPPORTUNITIES ⤚

- *January 8*—in ancient times, the feast day sacred to Justitia, Roman goddess of justice.
- Martin Luther King, Jr., Day—a movable date celebrating the birth and life of the famed civil rights and peace leader.
- *January 25*—St. Paul's Day, honoring the Christian apostle who was once a persecutor of the followers of Jesus until his dramatic conversion. He was executed in Rome, ca. 65 C.E.
- *February 3*—date of execution by lethal injection of Karla Faye Tucker in Huntsville, Texas, 1998.
- *February 10*—Nelson Mandela was released after 27 years in a South African prison, 1990.
- *February 14*—Saint Valentine's Day, commemorating the rebel priest who was executed by beheading on this day, 270 C.E.
- *February 22*—Roman festival day known as *Charistia*, honoring the goddess Concordia, who represented the principle of harmonious relations with all. It followed the Roman *Feralia* (February 21) when the spirits of the dead were believed to be abroad in the

world. On Charistia, people attempted to reconcile their differences and settle disputes.

- *March 1*—International Death Penalty Abolition Day, marks the anniversary of the date in 1847 when Michigan became the first English-speaking territory in the world to abolish capital punishment officially. According to Citizens United for Alternatives to the Death Penalty (CUADP), Abolition Day is a time to "remember the victims of violent crime and their survivors; it is a day to remember those killed by state sanctioned violence—guilty or not—and their survivors; and it is a day for intensified education and action for alternatives to the death penalty."

- *Good Friday*—movable date commemorating the execution by crucifixion of Jesus of Nazareth, ca. 33 C.E. Pageants, artwork, music, ritual, and theatrical reenactments of his arrest, condemnation, and execution are traditional in many places around the world.

- *Mother's Day*—springtime holiday, initiated in the early 1870s by Julia Ward Howe, as an international day of women's activism and advocacy for peace. (This festival was unrelated to the national day honoring mothers, later proposed by Anna Jarvis.) The Church of Gethsemane in Brooklyn, New York, has revived Howe's day as a time to educate the public about the plight of women in prison and to advocate for prison reform.

- *May 9, 11, 13*—in Roman times, three days known as *Lemuria*, when the spirits of the dead would revisit their former homes.

- *May 20*—annual anti-death penalty vigil held in Richmond, Virginia, to commemorate the 1992 execution of Roger Keith Coleman, whose appeal had been filed late and was thus deemed "procedurally defaulted."

- *May 30*—Joan of Arc executed by burning, 1431.

- *June 1*—festival day sacred to Carna, Roman goddess of doors and locks; the Norse goddess Syn, the includer and excluder; and of Tempestas, goddess of the storm.

- *June 19*—date of 1953 execution by electrocution of Julius and Ethel Rosenberg at Sing Sing prison in Ossining, New York, 1953; also, "Juneteenth," commemorating the day, in 1865, when African slaves in Texas finally learned that they had been legally free since January 1, 1863.

- *August 23*—date of execution by electrocution, in 1927, of Sacco and Vanzetti.
- *August 28*—date of Dr. Martin Luther King, Jr.'s, "I Have a Dream" speech before 250,000 at the March on Washington for Jobs, Peace and Freedom, 1963
- *September 13*—the Attica Prison uprising ended on this date, with the deaths of thirty-seven prisoners and nine guards, 1971.
- *October 31*—All Hallow's Eve, Halloween, originally the Celtic festival *Samhain*, a time to remember and honor the dead, and, in Mexico, combining Christian and Aztec traditions, *Dia de los Muertos* (The Day of the Dead), a festival during which life and death embrace, and skeletons dance.
- *November 19*—date of the execution by firing squad of Joe Hill, labor organizer and songwriter, in Utah, 1915.
- *December 8*—sacred feast day of Astraea, a Greek goddess of justice.
- *December 10*—Human Rights Day
- *December 23*—on the Celtic tree calendar, a blank day called Secret of the Unhewn Stone, a time to celebrate the quality of potential in all things.

Action as Witness

Death Watch Vigil

❖ *Monday, January 28, 2002: It's close to 3 P.M. and I'm all bundled up in multiple layers of clothing and socks in preparation for tonight's vigil outside of San Quentin. Tonight's temperatures are supposed to drop into the 30s, and I know from past experience that there is no place colder in this whole region than SQ Prison with its harsh winds off the bay. . . . I looked in the* San Francisco Chronicle *this morning to see what had been written about tonight's planned execution of Stephen Wayne Anderson. Not one article. Has it gotten to this? That executing a man is no longer news? Fortunately I turned to the Op-Ed page and there it was: an excellent commentary written by Bell Gale Chevigny. . . .*

3 A.M.: Well, Stephen's life was snuffed out at 12:32 A.M. What a loss. There were between 250–300 people who stood for hours on a very cold night to say this is not the way to run a society. We listened to anti-death penalty abolitionists, the father of a 21-year-old murder victim, clergy and religious, folk singers and many others who encouraged us not to give up the fight. We heard Stephen Wayne Anderson's spiritual director read his poems with tears pouring down her face. We stood with our hands raised in a blessing on Stephen as midnight came and went. We listened to the heartbeat of the drum and the wailing cries of a Native American man as we waited for official word of Stephen's death. It was powerful, sad and comforting all at the same time.

~PATRICIA LAY-DORSEY

Prayer Vigil

In December, 2000, Father Bryan Brooks, coordinator of prison ministry with the Catholic Diocese of Tulsa, put out a call to people of faith and goodwill to show opposition to capital punishment by attending a series of vigils. In a letter, published by the Oklahoma Coalition to Abolish the Death Penalty (OCADP), the priest explained:

> As we as the Church are preparing this Advent season to celebrate the birth of Christ, we as the state of Oklahoma are preparing in January and February to make history. Beginning in January, 2001, a total of nine Oklahoma death row inmates will be executed in a period of less than thirty days. . . . Never before has Oklahoma carried out this number of death sentences in so short a time.

In his letter, Father Brooks listed the expected execution dates and information about each of the condemned, and asked that people gather for prayer vigils at the front gate of the Oklahoma State Penitentiary in McAlester on the evenings of the executions. The prayers would be offered for the condemned inmates, the murder victims, their families, and for the corrections officers charged with carrying out the death sentence. Those unable to meet at the prison gates were asked to host vigils in their home churches and to ring church bells on the evenings of the executions or decorate their church doors with black cloth so that the executions would not pass by without notice.

> ❖ *I believe human beings are not violent by nature. Unlike lions and tigers, we are not naturally equipped to kill with sharp teeth and claws. From a Buddhist viewpoint, I believe that the basic nature of every sentient being is pure, that the deeper nature of mind is something pure. Human beings become violent because of negative thoughts which arise as a result of their environment and circumstance.*

~HIS HOLINESS THE DALAI LAMA, 1999

Solitary Vigil

❖ *It was the third vigil I have attended to mark the execution of a prisoner in California: a cold February night. . . . I felt it was important that the execution should not be just another day or that it pass unnoticed. . . . An execution is about missed opportunities: the opportunities of the prisoner and the victims; the opportunities of society; the opportunities of those who know the prisoner. . . . By the time an execution takes place, everything has been said. Those who come to the gates of San Quentin are set in their beliefs. . . .*

I preferred to stand at the gate and watch the lights in the upper stories of the North Block unit, where the death chamber is located. At that point, the execution is deeply personal. The State is about to kill one of my clients.

By the time the execution is set, the most powerful statement I can make is my silent observation. To bear witness at the gates, watching the row of guards, watching the movement inside the prison, watching the lights near the execution chamber. The speeches got in the way.

~ARNOLD ERICKSON

Ongoing Vigil

Across the country, anti-death penalty activists hold weekly or monthly vigils intended to remind passersby of the injustice of capital punishment. Two Catholic Worker houses in Baltimore—Viva House and Jonah House, sponsor vigils every Monday at various prison sites in the city. In Brooklyn, the Religious Society of Friends (Quakers), have maintained a silent anti-death penalty vigil near the borough's Supreme Court building every week for years.

II. NONVIOLENT NONCOOPERATION

❖ *It may seem a strange thing to begin a book with:—This book is not for any one who has time to read it—but the meaning of it is: this reading is good only as a preparation for work. If it is not to inspire life and work, it is bad.*

~FLORENCE NIGHTINGALE, *NOTES ON NURSING*, 1859

According to Gene Sharp in volume 2 of *The Politics of Nonviolent Action*, when activists use methods of noncooperation they "deliberately withdraw the usual forms and degree of their cooperation with the person, activity, institution, or regime with which they have become engaged in conflict." Following are examples of noncooperation used toward dismantling the execution machinery in the United States.

❖ *We need to keep the death penalty in the world's headlights, whether it be by talking with German companies that are thinking of building factories in death penalty states, or by having protests outside American businesses in Germany, or by protesting when American politicians who oversee executions visit Germany.*

~MICHAEL L. RADELET

Economic Actions

Boycott of a Death Penalty State
The Canadian Coalition Against the Death Penalty (CCADP) initiated an International Tourist Boycott of Texas in December, 1998. This was to protest the pending execution of Joseph Stanley Faulder. The group expressed outrage that then-Governor George W. Bush and other officials in Texas had disregarded the international obligation, as outlined in Article 36 of the "Vienna Convention on Consular Relations," to inform Faulder of his right to contact the Canadian consulate at the time of his arrest. In fact, for fifteen years the Canadian government was not aware that a Canadian citizen was under sentence of death in Texas.

In a letter to Governor Bush, CCADP wrote:

> We are surprised that you would put the positive relations between our two countries at risk. The European Union was thinking about an economic boycott, and if you allow this execution to take place, we will certainly begin a well publicized tourist boycott of Texas.
>
> "Texas: It's like a whole other country" is the phrase you use on your tourist posters. We are beginning to believe it's like a lot of other countries—Iran, Iraq, and the Sudan—some of the only other countries that insist on retaining capital punishment, and even these would certainly hesitate before killing a citizen of Canada.

In organizing the protest against Texas, CCADP widened the dialogue beyond the usual abolitionist groups to include various human rights groups, student groups, politicians, and travel agents. The boycott even got Texans talking to each other about the death penalty in

Artist: Eleanor Mill

the press and on radio talk shows. Activists from Italy, Germany, France, and Denmark joined in the effort to, as one bumper sticker read, BOYCOTT TEXAS—EXECUTION CAPITAL OF THE WESTERN WORLD. Lending his support for the boycott was Rubin "Hurricane" Carter, the executive director of the Association in Defense of the Wrongly Convicted. The former boxer, who spent nineteen years locked up for a murder many believe he did not commit, said that Texas was "loading up the prisons with illiterate people, loading them up with the disenfranchised, loading them up with the disadvantaged."

Ultimately, Stanley Faulder was executed on June 17, 1999.

Boycott of Pharmaceutical Manufacturers
In 1989, the Endeavor Project, an activist group of Texas death row prisoners, called for a boycott of the Abbott Laboratories and Organon Pharmaceuticals, and a petition drive to protest the company supplying Texas with Sodium Thiopental and Pavulon—drugs used in lethal injections. Both corporations claimed ignorance, stating first that they had no knowledge that the drugs they manufactured were being used

for executions in Texas; and second, that, even so, "we're not responsible for how our buyers use the drugs."

In an article in *The Endeavor: Live Voices from Death Row*, February–May, 1990, Robert West (prisoner number 731), wrote,

> As humanitarians and abolitionists, we must also hold all involved, every link in the chain, accountable for their part that feeds the killing machine, otherwise we are merely armchair activists and giving lip service to a cause that must have action in order to move forward and make a difference. Please join the boycott against Abbott Laboratories and Organon Pharmaceuticals. The cycle of violence must end. . . . Please return your signed petitions back to me to be recorded and forwarded to the companies.

The man who wrote these words was executed by lethal injection on July 27, 1997.

Boycott of Medical Professionals

In 1994, Physicians for Human Rights and the American College of Physicians launched a campaign aimed at discouraging doctors and other medical professionals from taking part in executions by administering lethal injections. Some states actually require the presence, if not the actual participation, of health-care professionals in the death chambers.

"It is hypocritical for health professionals to be involved in the death of individuals, instead of promoting health and life," said Abe Bonowitz, director of the Florida-based Citizens United Against the Death Penalty.

Boycott of Drug Distributors

When Human Rights Watch informed Joel Tate, the chief executive of McAlester Regional Health Center in McAlester, Oklahoma, that his hospital was the Oklahoma Department of Corrections's sole supplier of potassium chloride, Tate was in shock. He had believed he was in the business of saving lives, but potassium chloride is one of three drugs used in lethal injection executions. In June, 2001, as part of a new plan of action to defy death and dismantle the execution machinery in the

United States, Human Rights Watch urged Tate to sever his hospital's drug supply relationship with the prisons. The executive complied, ordering an immediate end of the sale of potassium chloride to corrections officials. This was the first success in a new anti-death penalty campaign to pressure pharmaceutical companies and drug distributors that provide lethal injection drugs by threatening negative publicity.

Human Rights Watch also instituted a letter-writing campaign directed at Bergen Brunswig Corporation and Cardinal Health, two California companies, to protest their complicity in supplying lethal drugs for executions.

Jeff Garis, executive director of Pennsylvania Abolitionists United Against the Death Penalty, said in a *Mother Jones* article, "This is not going to be the one key in ending the death penalty. It is part of a larger overall strategy, that is going to take multiple tactics and campaigns."

"Drug companies are in the business of making drugs for health and well-being, not to kill people," Steve Hawkins, executive director of the National Coalition to Abolish the Death Penalty, was quoted as saying. "If a department of corrections wants to be in the business of killing people, let it be expensive and let it be difficult."

Tax Resistance
David Nuttall, a war-tax resister in Delaware, protested his state's death penalty in 1981 and in subsequent years. He informed the Delaware Division of Revenue that he was more than willing to pay his taxes, but that he refused to allow his money to be used for killing. He was bound, he explained, to follow a higher imperative dictated by his conscience and his faith. He sent copies of his letters to his state legislators and to the governor.

More successful than he had ever hoped to be, Nuttall learned that one of his state representatives had forwarded the letter to the Director of Revenue who offered to intervene personally, reassigning Nuttall's income-tax checks by depositing them in the state's Revenue Refund Account, which is used only for refunding tax overpayments. By specifying this money, the administrator was able to guarantee that Nuttall would not be financially compromised in the deliberate taking of human life by the state through the death penalty.

After a decade of successfully negotiating to have his tax monies diverted in this way, Nuttall wrote in an article in the *Nonviolent Activist:*

I might not now, after eleven years of war tax refusal, feel energetic enough to begin to stand up against the death penalty, if I weren't already committed. But for me, the point is that where I had the energy to take a principled stand, I was reckless enough to try, and now it's personally compelling for me to continue to respond, year after year. It has changed the way I view myself, others, and my world; made me more thoughtful, more empowered, more creative; and prompted my choice of a community economic development degree and career.

III. NONVIOLENT INTERVENTION
ACTIONS THAT DISRUPT BUSINESS AS USUAL

According to Gene Sharp, methods of nonviolent intervention differ from the tactics categorized as protest and persuasion, and of noncooperation in that such methods

> operate both negatively and positively: they may disrupt, and even destroy, established behavior patterns, policies, relationships, or institutions which are seen as objectionable; or they may establish new behavior patterns, policies, relationships, or institutions which are preferred.

Fasting

Annual Fast

Starvin' for Justice is an annual event organized by the Abolitionist Action Committee (AAC), an ad-hoc group committed to educating the public about alternatives to the death penalty through nonviolent direct action. Since 1994, this four-day Fast & Vigil to Abolish the Death Penalty has taken place from June 29 to July 2 in front of the United States Supreme Court Building, in Washington, D.C. The dates are significant. June 29 is the anniversary of the 1972 *Furman v. Georgia* decision in which the Supreme Court found that the death penalty was being applied in an arbitrary and capricious manner. All states were then forced to suspend executions, reduce the sentences of people on death row, and rewrite the death penalty laws. July 2 is the anniversary of the 1976 *Gregg v. Georgia* decision, which allowed executions to resume in the United States.

Over the years, this event has steadily grown. Today, a number of organizations pitch in to help with funds and logistics for the Fast & Vigil. Overnight accommodations are generally provided by the Community for Creative Nonviolence, a homeless shelter with a room designated for people doing advocacy work. Participants in the vigil are encouraged to engage in public outreach (by leafleting, staffing the information table, talking with passersby) and to maintain a physical presence at the Court. The fast, for those who choose to participate, begins after a communal "last meal" on June 28, and, although fasting is not required, everyone is requested to refrain from eating or discussing food at the vigil site.

❖ *If you think you are too small to make a difference, try sleeping in a small room with a mosquito.*

~AFRICAN PROVERB

Execution Day Fast

Jonathan Nobles, age 37, made the conscious decision to forgo his "last meal" and, instead, fasted on October 7, 1998—the day of his execution in Huntsville, Texas. He asked only for the wine and wafer of Holy Communion. According to Bishop Edmond Carmody, who had visited the prisoner for six years and was there to witness the execution, Nobles called his last communion "spiritual food for the journey home."

Nobles was executed on the "feast of the Holy Rosary," a day celebrated by Roman Catholics. Strapped to the lethal injection gurney, the condemned man turned to look at those who had gathered to witness the execution. At that point, according to Bishop Carmody, "we held up our rosaries so he could see them and know that we were praying for him. That brought joy to his face, to know that we were there with him."

Execution Vigil Fast

In October, 1998, when the Nebraska Supreme Court announced the execution date of January 14 for Randolph Reeves, activist-artist Marylyn Felion began a liquids-only fast "in sorrow and repentance for the monstrous evil of the death penalty."

Felion, who had been a witness to the 1997 execution of Robert Williams, issued a press release in which she wrote:

In a democracy, we are all responsible for the actions of the state. Therefore, in a democracy which still uses the death penalty, we are all executioners. We all have our hands on the switch. By this fast I want to make it as clear as possible that I am removing my hand from this switch. I offer this fast in sorrow and repentance for whatever I have done, or failed to do, that has allowed this evil to continue.

Inmate Hunger Strikes

Texas—In April, 1989, inmates on death row in Texas launched an "Indefinite and Continuous Chain Hunger Strike" to protest the discriminatory application of the death penalty, the use of unethical law-enforcement tactics, and the ongoing abuse of death row prisoners. Two prisoners at a time pledged not to eat for a period of fourteen days. Then, another two prisoners would take the next fourteen-day period. The prisoners, who began this action from a point of deprivation, experienced serious physical and mental repercussions, such as dehydration, delirium, and drastic weight loss.

Sympathetic people outside the prison were encouraged to write to the fasters, to boost their morale with notes of encouragement. They were also invited to participate in a Symbolic Solidarity Fast on the first and fifteenth days of each month, in support of the primary hunger strike, and send their names to the inmates' newsletter.

Pennsylvania—In March, 1998, approximately fifty inmates on death row at SCI-Green Prison in Waynesburg (home, at that time, of Mumia Abu-Jamal) began a hunger strike to protest new rules, thought to be instituted in retribution for a series of lawsuits brought against prison guards for brutality. The new regulations limited inmate personal property to two orange-crate-sized boxes (for most death row prisoners, legal papers alone take up more space than that), severely restricted family visits and phone calls, banned food in the cells, and forced the removal of all family photos and mementos.

Civil rights groups and anti-death penalty activists augmented the prisoners' hunger strike by making thousands of daily phone calls to prison officials. According to one report, the prison's fax machine was so flooded with messages in support of the hunger strikers, that its number had to be changed. The strike was effective in calling attention to the brutal conditions at the prison and in inspiring prison reformers to keep up their efforts.

Florida—In April, 2000, an eight-day hunger strike was staged by 250 death row inmates at the Florida State Prison in Starke. This was in response to the proposal by prison officials to ban physical contact during family visits and to remove all arts-and-crafts supplies from inmates' cells. The proposal outraged the family members of the inmates. Janice Figueroa, the mother of inmate Bobby Raleigh, said, "The human touch is a necessary thing for every living person. Just because he is on death row doesn't mean my motherly instincts have changed."

After hearing of the proposed policy change, the families of the condemned formed the Florida Death Row Advocacy Group. Jacquelynne Perry, the wife of a condemned man, said, "They are sitting in little cages about the size of your bathroom. It is good for them to stay creative and busy."

The hunger strike ended when one inmate attempted, unsuccessfully, to hang himself in his cell. In a suicide note he wrote,

> I, Jesus Delgado, #658187, prefer to die before accepting this stupid rule that is senseless. If I cannot kiss or hug my dearest mother and my family members, then what sense is [*sic*] my corporal existence have in this world. The fact that we have been condemned to die does not signify that we are to be entombed alive in a building.

Texas—In 2001, Roy Pippin, a white death row inmate, went on a thirty-five-day water-only hunger strike, to protest prison conditions. The Texas death row had been moved to a maximum security prison called the Polunsky Unit the year before, in response to a November, 1998, escape by seven inmates. In an article, Pippin wrote about the move to the new death row:

> The treatment we received when being loaded on buses for the trip to this unit showed me what we were in for. No animal could have that inhumane type of treatment without the public or authorities stepping in to stop the abuse immediately. . . . The trip over had grown men crying and gritting their teeth in pain. . . . I knew right then that we were headed to hell on earth. I was absolutely correct.

At the Polunsky Unit, the inmates routinely suffered sleep deprivation since they were awakened by flashlight checks for *hourly* prisoner counts. Breakfast was served at 3 A.M. Food portions had been reduced. All personal belongings had to fit into two shopping bags. There were no televisions, no religious services, and few health-care provisions. (In March, 2001, Eddie Rowton died in his cell of a heart attack after two days of begging for medical attention. According to witnesses, his pleas were ignored.)

Yolanda Torres, a lawyer from Riverside, Texas, said in a report, "Conditions on Texas death row are atrocious. Inmates are enclosed in tiny confined cubicles that are more like boxes than cells and condemned to virtual sensory deprivation. They are slowly being driven crazy."

Gary Taylor, another death row lawyer, said, "I've seen a marked deterioration in the mental state of my clients since the move from Ellis. The attitude among most Texans is they don't want convicted murderers living in a country club. But many would be appalled if they knew what is going on."

Pippin ended his hunger strike on the last day of 2001, having successfully drawn some attention to the inmates' plight at the Polunsky Unit.

Solidarity Hunger Strikes

At age seventeen, after committing a number of robberies, Gary Graham (a.k.a. Shaka Sankofa) was convicted of the murder of a white drug dealer. There was no physical evidence linking him to the scene of the crime. The sole "eyewitness" had first said that the black youth was not the killer, but, when called by the prosecution at the trial, told a different story. The court-appointed lawyer made little attempt to defend his client, nor did he call the three eyewitnesses who would have testified that the wrong man was on trial. (Later, upon hearing this news, several jurors filed affidavits saying they would not have voted to convict if all the evidence had been presented.) It was a weak case at best, full of unanswered questions, but it ended in a sure sentence of death.

Graham/Sankofa spent the next nineteen years on death row in Texas where he learned to read. Eventually, he founded the Endeavor

Project, a prison-activist group that published a newsletter, and became an articulate critic of the criminal justice system.

In June, 2000, a five-day hunger strike was launched in Detroit by the congregations of the Central United Church and the New Bethel Baptist Church. Participating in the hunger strike were religious, labor, and community leaders who joined an international effort to pressure then-governor George W. Bush to halt the Texas execution.

The Michigan hunger strikers set up camp outside the Detroit City Council building where they distributed anti-death penalty literature, answered questions, and asked passersby, on foot and in cars, to sign petitions protesting the pending execution. Noon-hour rallies effectively garnered media coverage from local TV, radio, and newspapers.

Despite the efforts of these and many other anti-death penalty activists, Graham/Sankofa was executed on June 22, 2000. He struggled every step of the way to the death chamber, protesting his innocence. As witnessed by Reverend Jesse Jackson, the condemned man screamed, "They are killing me tonight! They are murdering me tonight," before his voice was silenced by lethal chemicals.

Physical Obstruction, Invasion, and Occupation

Blocking the Governors' Mansions
As Malvina Reynolds made clear in her 1964 protest song, (a song later embellished and made famous by Judy Collins), blocking doorways isn't nice. Blocking doorways is, however, a tried-and-true nonviolent tactic, useful for disrupting business as usual.

In April of 2000, over five hundred anti-death penalty activists in Pennsylvania encircled the Governor's mansion with bright-yellow tape bearing the words, CRIME SCENE—DO NOT CROSS—CRIME SCENE—DO NOT CROSS.

In Austin, Texas, in the spring of 2000, some three hundred and fifty people surrounded the Governor's mansion in Austin, demanding that George W. Bush stop all executions and declare a moratorium. They chanted, "Governor Death, you can't hide! / We've got justice on our side," and "No Justice! No Peace! / Moratorium now!"

Using Chains
Harrisburg, Pennsylvania—On May 1, 1999, after staging a large demonstration in the capital, two hundred and fifty people marched to

the governor's mansion, demanding a moratorium on the death penalty. Once there, twelve activists chained themselves to the gates, effectively blocking all entrances.

Philadelphia—On August 1, 2000, a hot, summer day of press conferences and rallies by anti-death penalty organizers, four thousand protesters marched through the streets of the city, then host to the Republican National Convention. In an action called "Crashing the Executioner's Ball," they stopped traffic in the center of the city, blocked intersections by chaining themselves together, and threw debris into the streets. In a statement, some of the protesters called it a "day of repudiation of the death penalty, the frame-up of Mumia Abu-Jamal, and the entire criminal justice system." Over four hundred and fifty people were arrested, including some who had been in a warehouse making puppets—one for each person executed in Texas while George W. Bush was governor.

Angel Action
At the April 1999 trial of one of the men accused of murdering gay college student Matthew Shepard, in Laramie, Wyoming, Shepard's friends staged an "Angel Action." Donning gauzy white gowns and oversized, upraised angel wings, they stood silently outside the courthouse, gently but effectively blocking the harsh sight of anti-gay demonstrators who carried signs that read GOD HATES FAGS.

17-Minute Blockade
In Oslo, Norway, during rush hour on April 14, 1999, people protesting the death sentence of Mumia Abu-Jamal pulled a police fence into the busy street in front of the United States Embassy. They effectively blocked the street for seventeen minutes—one minute for each year Abu-Jamal had spent on death row.

Action to Shut down a National Monument
On July 3, 1999, almost one hundred activists from around the country met in Philadelphia, in 100-degree heat, to bar visitor access to the Liberty Bell. They maintained that, "so long as Mumia Abu-Jamal is on death row, there is no true liberty in Pennsylvania."

The protesters handed out leaflets in Liberty Bell Pavilion, unfurled a large banner from the pavilion's roof that read FREEDOM RINGS FOR MUMIA, and formed a semicircle around the historic bell. Ninety-five protesters, including a woman in a wheelchair, committed civil disobedience, blocking the entrance doors and disrupting a busy tourist day. They sang as they were arrested. Across the street, other demonstrators maintained a legal vigil, shouted words of encouragement, and watched a street theater performance.

The action came after months of coalition work, bringing together diverse individuals and organizations for a common goal. Nonviolence training gave the participants practice in working together and making quick group-based decisions.

Rush-hour Protest

In September, 1999, one hundred spirited and noisy pro-Mumia activists blocked downtown Detroit intersections as well as the tunnel from Michigan to Canada. Young drummers from the Anti-Racist Action kept up a steady beat while other protesters distributed leaflets to passing cars.

Disruption of Fund-raiser

Carrying signs that read STOP THE EXECUTION OF GARY GRAHAM, and GOV. BUSH: DON'T KILL ANOTHER INNOCENT MAN, two women invaded the $1,000-a-plate fund-raiser for Bush at the Crowne Plaza Hotel in Palo Alto, California, just three days before the June, 2000, execution of Graham (a.k.a. Shaka Sankofa). Outside the hotel, a crowd of protesters called for a retrial.

❖ *In each of these actions involving civil disobedience, some creative sign, some aesthetic display (the lying prostrate, the die-in, the lit candle, the song, the artistic flyer, street theater, the chaining of one's body) accompanies the act of bodily confrontation. . . . They give the confrontation a quality of aesthetic display, the drama that drives the word* demonstration *into its full and original meaning,* monstrare, *to show, reveal. . . .*

Through artistic creation, resisters to the present order are allowed to taste the future, we might say, to feel themselves already in the future for which they work. Art has a capacity to re-present, *or make present, what it depicts.*

~MARK LEWIS TAYLOR

Occupation of Offices

On June 19, 2000, for one hour, six activists occupied the New York State Republican offices housing the "Bush for President" headquarters, while one thousand protesters marched through the streets of midtown Manhattan chanting "Death row, hell no! Free Gary Graham!" To the rousing rhythm of drums, they blocked traffic and shouted, "Free Shaka! Free Mumia!" The protesters objected to the reintroduction of the state's death penalty by Governor George Pataki and demanded that Republican leaders pressure George W. Bush to stop the execution of Graham/Sankofa.

Sit-In / Read-In

On June 16, 1999, fifty people, a mixed group of French, American, and African, invaded the American Library on a small street in Paris not far from the Eiffel Tower. They read aloud a manifesto addressed to President Bill Clinton who was dining in the city that night with President Jacques Chirac, demanding medical care for Mumia Abu-Jamal and other death row prisoners. Then they staged a sit-in and read aloud the prison writings of Abu-Jamal who had just been given the prestigious PEN International Literary Censorship Award. After an hour and a half, French police arrived in riot gear to arrest the demonstrators.

Storming the Barricades

Shouting "stop the legal lynching of Shaka Sankofa!," over one thousand people marched through the streets of Huntsville, Texas, then gathered outside the Walls Unit where Graham/Sankofa was being strapped down for lethal injection on June 22, 2000. Just minutes before the execution, they began to pound on the barricades. When a barrier was pushed down, a number of the protesters rushed through. Six young people and two long-time activists were arrested for the action. Television coverage later reported that they had "stormed the barricades."

With news of Graham/Sankofa's death, some protesters burned Texas and American flags as well as an effigy of George W. Bush.

Mock Newspaper Action

In the Bay Area, on April 14, 1999, thousands of copies of the *San Francisco Chronicle* were wrapped in a four-page mock newspaper called the *SF Chonicals*. The mock paper, printed in a style and typeface nearly identical to the *Chronicle*, featured anti-death penalty articles and background information on the case of Abu-Jamal. It also announced the "Millions for Mumia" march and rally scheduled in ten days.

IV. BUILDING THE NEW SOCIETY— ONE PAPER CLIP AT A TIME

In addition to the nonviolent actions discussed in this chapter, there are many other ways to do the work of changing the world. Most may not seem terribly exciting, but they are the stuff of real change.

Checkbook Activism

Citizens United for Alternatives to the Death Penalty (CUADP) encourages "checkbook activism" and has come up with some catchy ways to encourage contributions. One such effort was its "Pocket Change Challenge." In the fund-raising letter to its members, CUADP encouraged its 3,600 + supporters to pledge just two dollars a month. One of their members wrote back:

> It is hard to believe that a mere two dollars a month from each CUADP constituent could provide so much for CUADP's operation and administration. It truly is pocket change—giving up one coffee a month, or a bag of chips. It is such a simple concept that I am ashamed that I have not taken part in it until now. . . . All it takes is all of us to pitch in a little, instead of a few pitching in a lot.

Everyday Actions

Mark William Olson, a former editor of the faith-based magazine *The Other Side*, proposed eight practical actions against capital punishment. Written for Christian activists, the suggestions outlined below could be adapted by any concerned person.

(1) Practice forgiveness and grace at every opportunity

> When we seek to offer forgiveness, even in small things, every day of our lives, we are less likely to be caught up in any whirlwind of

hate. When we're people of grace, we'll be supportive of all victims of violence, whether it be murder or capital punishment or war or greed.

(2) Never vote for a government official who supports or condones capital punishment

(3) Establish a personal relationship with a person on death row

According to Olson, this could mean writing to the person every month "whether they're guilty or innocent," remembering them on their birthdays, sending money for special needs, accepting collect calls, and making personal visits. Organizations opposing the death penalty often have names and addresses of prisoners seeking correspondence.

(4) Help create a "culture of resistance"

> We can help create a "culture of resistance" by seeking to draw others into the kind of deep relationship with God that makes capital punishment unthinkable. We need to be evangelistic in our thinking, transforming an ever-wider circle of companions, always showing the spiritual basis of our concerns.

(5) Contribute financially to organizations that overturn death sentences

Olson recommends looking for groups that have "a high level of both political independence and legal expertise," and gives as an example the Equal Justice Initiative of Alabama, headquartered in Montgomery.

(6) Contribute financially to organizations that support the condemned and their families

Noting that "A death sentence is an emotional and spiritual blow not only to the condemned person but also to members of their family," Olson recommends giving support to groups like New Hope House in Griffin, Georgia.

(7) Educate yourself about the death penalty and contribute to educational and advocacy groups working against it

Whereas Olson suggests working with such deserving groups as the National Coalition to Abolish the Death Penalty, Amnesty International, and Murder Victims' Families for Reconciliation, he also has this warning:

> Beware, however, of organizations that suggest that the death penalty be replaced by life sentences without parole. That option is as unbiblical and un-Christian as capital punishment, for the God who raises the dead is also the God who frees the prisoner.

(8) Mourn for all those who are put to death

> Each time we mourn, we take on a little more of God's own Spirit. Each time we mourn, we gain a little more of the strength we need.
> Mourning for those who are killed can take the form of quiet prayer, heartfelt wailing, or deep interaction with Scripture. We can mourn individually or with friends, or family. But each time an execution occurs, we gain strength—and freedom—through mourning.

Assisting Those Defending the Indigent-Accused

In his thought-provoking essay "The Anti-Death Penalty Movement Has Failed," Andrew Hammel, a defense attorney, criticized abolitionists for presenting an unconvincing message to the American public. He made several suggestions for ways to improve the campaign against capital punishment, including: avoid bogus claims of innocence; do not make martyrs or heroes out of death row inmates; de-emphasize demonstrations. Most importantly, he recommended several support actions for advocates, such as the following:

- attend capital trials "to take notes on what happens and to counterbalance the devastatingly effective presence of victims' rights groups"
- develop an effective database of information on death row inmates, the costs of executions vs. life imprisonment, and so forth
- lobby for legislative reform with a "tough on crime, tough on the causes of crime, but easy on justice" program
- "help lawyers who are representing capital murder defendants at trial put together compelling cases in mitigation." Noting that funding for indigent death penalty defense is almost non-existent, Hammel suggested that, with the guidance and control of the trial

attorney, volunteers could "help locate and interview family members, teachers, and other witnesses who might be able to present favorable evidence about the defendant, and to track down hospital, school, and military records that could prove helpful."

V. ORGANIZING IN THE RELIGIOUS CONTEXT

❖ *The commandment "Thou Shalt Not Kill" does not have an asterisk next to it.*

~MICHAEL L. RADELET

Weekly Prayer for Those on Death Row

Every Sunday at the Church of Gethsemane (see "banner projects" earlier in this chapter), I join with the other worshipers to say a prayer for persons on death row. Each week we read over sixty names aloud. Doing this, it takes about a year to publicly lift in prayer the approximately 3,500 names of all the death row inmates in the United States. Then, we start over. (The complete text of the prayer can be found in Appendix 2, pages 169–70)

Sometimes the given names catch us by surprise. There is a Heck and a Holly (last name Wood), a Caesar and a Ulysses, a Jessie James and a John Wayne. There are also names with a religious ring to them. In Missouri there is a Moses, in Ohio, a Genesis. On North Carolina's death row there is a man named John Wesley (the founder of Methodism) and another named Yahweh (the name of God in the Judeo-Christian Bible). In Oklahoma there is an Emmanuel, in Alabama, a Jeremiah. In Florida there is both a Jesus and a Krishna (the name of the blue-skinned, flute-playing Hindu deity who is, ironically, an advocate of selfless action).

The recitation often gives us pause, conjuring, perhaps, young parents who put their best hopes and dreams into choosing just the right names for their babies. What happened? Why are men named Moses and Jesus sitting in death row cells the size of walk-in closets in 21st century America?

Devoting a portion of our Sunday worship to reciting the names of the condemned is one way the Church of Gethsemane makes visible the invisible and keeps the people on death row from fading into society's harsh sunset without a whisper of protest or lament. With the prayer for persons on death row, the church is saying, "You are not alone. We see you. We remember you."

After saying the prayer, the Gethsemane congregation stands to recite an affirmation of faith, the last line of which is, "We believe that people can change, and that God keeps pulling us to life, and to a new world of joy and peace." This line is said with extra emphasis, week after week, for good reason; the congregation is comprised of ex-prisoners, families of prisoners, and neighborhood people in solidarity with the poor and imprisoned. We know, firsthand, that people can change. We've done it. We've seen it. We believe it.

❖ *Not a one of us hasn't looked at a killer on TV or a monster of international politics and said we'd be better off if they were dead. But Jesus says love your enemy, pray for those who persecute you, turn your cheek—all these things that seem beyond us, like justice, mercy, and compassion. But if the Bible tells us anything, it tells us that God knows best, and the gospel is a guide and a beacon for our living. When we follow it we live. When we stray from it we stumble. Violence begets violence. Viciousness begets viciousness. A hard lesson for us—an easy lesson for God. "Let him who is without sin cast the first killing stone." God's wisdom still stops us in our tracks all these years later.*

~REVEREND DAVID DYSON

Religious Organizing against the Death Penalty Project

Noting that "nearly every large religious body in the United States has a strong statement condemning the death penalty," but lamenting that, "many religious people are unaware that their group has adopted such a statement," the criminal justice program of the American Friends Service Committee launched the Religious Organizing Against the Death Penalty Project—a coalition of faith-based activists. Its goal is to provide people of faith with the tools and resources needed to become effective advocates for the abolition of capital punishment. The project's organizing materials feature a statement by Sister Helen Prejean:

The role of the religious community is to reconcile what seems irreconcilable: love for death row inmates and their human dignity, and love for murder victims and their dignity and compassion for the hurt of their family members. Our spiritual energy can unite and combine what ideology alone can never bring together.

Some of the religiously oriented materials provided to groups include an organizing packet, *Dead Man Walking* study guides, a compilation of statements by national religious bodies about the death penalty, and educational videos. It also provides training at conferences.

❖ *It says in the Talmud that whenever anyone was executed by a court, God cried. God cried out, "My head hurts! My arm hurts! My head hurts!" . . . [I read in the* San Francisco Chronicle] *. . . an interview with Timothy McVeigh, who killed 168 people in Oklahoma City and wounded six hundred others. He was asked why he thought it was okay to resort to violence to further his cause. He said, "If government is the teacher, violence would be an acceptable option. What do we do when we go to war? What are we doing with the death penalty? It appears they use violence as an option all the time." . . . Take it from a man who killed 168 innocent souls in Oklahoma. Our actions have consequences and the only possible consequence of killing and hatred is more of the same. Every time we add another horror to the world, every time we add another death, God cries out, "My head hurts. My arm hurts. My head hurts," and the wheel keeps turning.*

~RABBI ALAN LEW

Amnesty International's
"Annual National Weekend of Faith in Action"

Each fall since 1997, Amnesty International has organized a "Faith in Action" weekend. These were some of the actions in 2002:

Alaska—In Anchorage, Alaskans Against the Death Penalty invited community leaders to read their faith statements against capital punishment and lead prayers at a rally in the town square.

Arizona—Participants at an Interfaith Vigil of Hope and Community in Phoenix followed a candle-lit path on a "walk of inspiration." An interfaith choir then sang at a Guided Prayer service.

California—California People of Faith Working Against the Death Penalty sponsored a speaking tour by Bud Welch, a death penalty opponent whose daughter was killed in the Oklahoma City Federal Building bombing.

Florida—Students at the LaSalle High School in Miami prepared resource packets about capital punishment for their religion teachers and government/law studies teachers.

Idaho—Young people from the Our Lady of the Rosary Church in Boise planned an action to draw a parallel of Jesus's walk to the crucifixion and of John Coffey's walk to the electric chair in Stephen King's novel *The Green Mile*.

New Jersey—A coalition of groups sponsored a two day Speak Out About the Death Penalty at Rutgers University Law School. There were panel discussions and workshops for the "religious community," the "community at large," and the "legal community."

IF JESUS HAD LIVED IN THE UNITED STATES...

Signe Wilkinson, *Philadelphia Daily News*

New Mexico—Several congregations included in their newsletters a petition by the New Mexico Coalition to Repeal the Death Penalty.

New York—The Bethany Presbyterian Church in Rochester held an open forum, "The Death Penalty—An Eye for an Eye."

Pennsylvania—A presentation titled "From Death Row to Freedom: Voices of Innocence" was presented at the York College chapel, featuring testimonies by three former inmates, exonerated for their crimes.

South Carolina—The Newman Catholic Fellowship and the Amnesty International chapter at Furman University in Greenville sponsored a screening of the movie *Dead Man Walking*.

Tennessee—The Episcopal Peace Fellowship in Nashville put a notice in the *Service Leaflet* requesting prayers remembering "all those who have died as a result of violence or government-imposed executions."

Texas—A criminal justice professor at Sam Houston State University spoke after a screening of *Balancing the Scales*, a documentary film that examines the issue of capital punishment and the movement to seek a moratorium on executions in Texas.

> ❖ *Remember those who are in prison, as though you were in prison with them; those who are being tortured, as though you yourselves were being tortured.*
>
> ~HEBREWS 13: 3

SOME GOOD NEWS FOR ACTIVISTS

A series of experiments in social psychology, conducted by Stanley Milgram at Yale University from 1960–1963, are of great significance for people involved in working against the death penalty. In his book *Obedience to Authority*, Milgram explained that he'd been inspired to study his topic in light of the Nazi extermination of European Jews:

> ... from 1933 to 1945 millions of innocent people were systematically slaughtered on command. Gas chambers were built, death

camps were guarded, daily quotas of corpses were produced with the same efficiency as the manufacture of appliances. These inhumane policies may have originated in the mind of a single person, but they could only have been carried out on a massive scale if a very large number of people obeyed orders.

Milgram devised his famous experiment:

A person comes to a psychological laboratory and is told to carry out a series of acts that come increasingly into conflict with conscience. The main question is how far the participant will comply with the experimenter's instructions before refusing to carry out the actions required of him.

Here's how Milgram's basic experiment works. Two people come to a psychology lab to take part in a study, supposedly of memory and learning. One is designated a "teacher," the other a "learner." An experimenter, who is actually the on-site authority figure, explains that the study is concerned with the effects of punishment on learning. The learner is then strapped into a chair, has an electrode attached to his/her wrist, and is given a list of word pairs to study.

The real focus of the experiment is the person assigned the task of being the "teacher" who is instructed to ask the learner questions. When the learner answers correctly, the volunteer continues on to the next question. When the learner answers incorrectly, however, the volunteer is instructed to administer an electric shock. The shocks increase with each incorrect answer. They range from very slight (about 15 volts) to moderate, strong, very strong, intense, extreme, and dangerous. The last degree indicated on the dial is simply labeled "XXX." The assumption is that the shock could be lethal. As explained by Milgram,

The "teacher" is a genuinely naive subject who has come to the laboratory to participate in an experiment. The learner, or victim, is an actor who actually receives no shock at all. The point of the experiment is to see how far a person will proceed in a concrete and measurable situation in which he is ordered to inflict increasing pain on a protesting victim. At what point will the subject refuse to obey the experimenter?

The results of this study were discouraging and depressing.

> Despite the fact that many subjects experience stress, despite the fact that many protest to the experimenter, a substantial proportion continue to the last shock on the generator. . . .
>
> This is, perhaps, the most fundamental lesson of our study: ordinary people, simply dong their jobs, and without any particular hostility on their part, can become agents in a terrible destructive process.

Add to this bad news another disturbing observation. The man who originally played the part of the learner/victim was described by Milgram as "a forty-seven year old accountant, trained for the role; he was of Irish-American descent and most observers found him mild-mannered and likable." They may have found him likable, but after administering the shocks many subjects seemed to turn against him:

> Such comments as, "He was so stupid and stubborn he deserved to get shocked," were common. Once having acted against the victim, these subjects found it necessary to view him as an unworthy individual, whose punishment was made inevitable by his own deficiencies of intellect and character.

Much has been written about the Milgram study and its significance. It made it abundantly clear that it was not just the Germans of World War II era who had a problem blindly obeying orders. The good Americans participating in the Yale study were not risking personal harm. Even so, they capitulated quickly when instructed by an authority figure and turned up the dial, ignoring the learner's screams.

Many variations of the Milgram experiment were conducted, most of them equally discouraging. There was one, however, which proved a bright note in the midst of the darkness, though it received little attention. It is one that holds encouraging implications for death penalty abolitionists.

This variation is thus described by Milgram,

> The strategy is to replicate the basic experiment, but with this difference: the subject is placed in the midst of two peers who defy the experimenter and refuse to punish the victim against his will.

In what degree will the pressure created by their actions affect the naive subject's behavior?

At the point of administering the 150-volt (strong) shock level, the first teacher stood up and walked away and sat in another part of the room. At the 210-volt (very strong) shock level, the second teacher got up, expressing concern for the "learner" and said, in accordance with the script, "I am not willing to shock that man against his will. I'll have no part of it."

The results of this Milgram-experiment variation were very different from the original study. The majority of subjects left soon after the two peers refused to administer the painful test.

According to Milgram,

> The effects of peer rebellion are very impressive in undercutting the experimenter's authority. Indeed, of the score of experimental variations completed in this study, none was so effective in undercutting the experimenter's authority as the manipulation reported here.

The significance of this study is clear. Most people will go along, obedient to authority, even when they are asked to do something they don't believe is right, unless someone else sets an example of questioning that authority.

The good news for activists is that this study illustrates the power of setting an example. It heralds the importance of risking lone action, of speaking up even when all seems lost, for clearly we are influenced by each other, even as we feel pulled to obey authority. It is possible to revive another's conscience, to require another to stop and think and change direction. What the Milgram variation tells us is that it is the process of taking courageous action that matters, even when we cannot know for sure that our actions will do any good.

⫸ **6** ⫷

Let It Get under Your Skin
(make it personal)

✒ Excerpts from "The Ballad of Reading Gaol" by Oscar Wilde

In 1895, Irish playwright and author Oscar Wilde, famous as a wit, maverick, and free spirit, was imprisoned for homosexual "offenses." After his release in 1897, and greatly subdued, Wilde moved to France where he wrote this poem, published in 1898. Wilde died two years later at the age of forty-six. The following are excerpts from this lengthy ballad, describing the sympathy one prisoner feels for another, condemned to hang, who is in an adjacent exercise yard.

from I

. . . . I never saw a man who looked
With such a wistful eye
Upon that little tent of blue
Which prisoners call the sky,
And at every drifting cloud that went
With sails of silver by.

I walked, with other souls in pain,
Within another ring,
And was wondering if the man had done
A great or little thing,
When a voice behind me whispered low,
"That fellow's got to swing". . . .

from II

. . . The oak and elm have pleasant leaves
That in the spring-time shoot:
But grim to see is the gallows-tree,
With its alder-bitten root,
And, green or dry, a man must die
Before it bears its fruit!

The loftiest place is the seat of grace
For which all worldlings try:
But who would stand in hempen band
Upon a scaffold high,
And through a murderer's collar take
His last look at the sky?

It is sweet to dance to violins
When Love and Life are fair:
To dance to flutes, to dance to lutes
Is delicate and rare:
But it is not sweet with nimble feet
To dance upon the air! . . .

from III

. . . .We waited for the stroke of eight:
Each tongue was thick with thirst;
For the stroke of eight is the stroke of Fate
That makes a man accursed,
And Fate will use a running noose
For the best man and the worst.

We had no other thing to do,
Save to wait for the sign to come;
So, like things of stone in a valley lone,
Quiet we sat and dumb;
But each man's heart beat thick and quick,
Like a madman on a drum!

With sudden shock the prison-clock
Smote on the shivering air,
And from all the gaol rose up a wail
Of impotent despair,
Like the sound the frightened marshes hear
From some leper in his lair.

And as one sees most fearful things
In the crystal of a dream,
We saw the greasy hempen rope
Hooked to the blackened beam,
And heard the prayer the hangman's snare
Strangled into a scream. . . .

from IV

There is no chapel on the day
On which they hang a man:
The Chaplain's heart is far too sick,
Or his face is far too wan,
Or there is that written in his eyes
Which none should look upon.

So they kept us close till nigh on noon,
And then they rang the bell,
And the warders with their jingling keys
Opened each listening cell,
And down the iron stair we tramped,
Each from his separate Hell.

Out into God's sweet air we went,
But not in wonted way,
For this man's face was white with fear,
And that man's face was gray,
And I never saw sad men who looked
So wistfully at the day.

I never saw sad men who looked
With such a wistful eye

Upon that little tent of blue
We prisoners called the sky,
And at every happy cloud that passed
In such strange freedom by. . . .

from V

I know not whether Laws be right,
Or whether Laws be wrong;
All that we know who lie in gaol
Is that the wall is strong;
And that each day is like a year,
A year whose days are long. . . .

Meditate on the Details

❖ *Easily supported in theory, execution loses its allure up close, where the troubling details of our humanity are more distinct.*
~MICHAEL A. MELLO

On my fiftieth birthday, I had a party. My apartment was filled with friends who sang folk songs and Broadway show tunes around my piano and read original poems written for me. It was an evening of laughter, music, hugs, and chocolate cake with raspberries on top. I was acutely aware of the abundance and good fortune that graces my life.

At the time, I was actively writing this book. The people on death row were on my mind, even on this happy occasion. It occurred to me that one way to get past the overwhelming statistics to the personal, would be to choose just such a momentous day in my life, and see if, while I was experiencing such joy, someone was being led to their death. Life. Death. Joy. Despair. Was someone being killed while friends sang "Happy Birthday" to me?

A few days later, I searched the Internet to see if anyone had been executed on my birthday night. That was when I read about Mark Andrew Fowler.

In the picture on the Web site, Mark appears as a mustachioed man with receding blond hair, bags under his eyes, and a forced grin. Here's what I learned about the man who was executed on my fiftieth birthday.

One night in 1985, he and a friend killed three night-shift employees at a grocery store. The next night, he had a party and served steaks stolen from the store. Mark eventually came to regret the murders and the party. He also regretted bringing shame and pain to his family, especially after another tragedy struck his family.

While Mark was on death row, his 83-year-old paternal grandmother was raped and murdered. Robert Miller, Jr., confessed to the crimes and was sentenced to death. Seven years later, however, DNA cleared Miller. He had made a false confession. Another man had done the crime. Alarmed at how close they had come to executing an innocent man, Mark's father said, "It was after that when I really thought, Christ's sake, what does all this killing do? We could've killed an innocent man. If we would've killed him, we never would have known that he was innocent."

Mark's father, who was both the son of a murder victim and the father of a murderer, must have been bewildered by the hand life had dealt him. "I'm on both sides of the issue," he said. "I could be a hate-monger and want to get back at everyone, but that wouldn't do anything. When Mark is executed, Oklahoma will not be one bit safer than it is today. And killing someone won't bring Mom back, either." The week before his son's execution, he kept busy making a small wooden box to hold his son's ashes. "It's a labor of love, and it's beautiful," he said.

In addition to having the support of his father, Mark Fowler had many friends in Tulsa's Roman Catholic community. He was the nephew of Father Gregory Gier, rector of Holy Family Cathedral, one of the city's largest Catholic churches. At Mark's clemency hearing, held days before the execution, four busloads of death penalty opponents came to show support. Archbishop Eusebius J. Beltran addressed the Pardon and Parole Board, pleading for Mark's life. "To execute Mark Fowler is to cut short the penance and conversion he needs to make," argued the Archbishop. He said,

> To execute Mark Fowler does not rectify the wrong that he did. Executing Mark Fowler only perpetuates the violence and evil he perpetrated. The fact that we are the only country [sic] in the western hemisphere to continue to impose the death penalty should raise certain fundamental questions. Is this the best that we

can do? Or does an execution simply return evil for evil? When we do return evil for evil, we degrade ourselves. . . . The power of forgiveness is real. It heals the forgiver and communicates God's mercy to the sinner. Please, find it in your hearts to grant clemency to Mark Fowler. In this instance you have the power of life or death. Choose life.

On my birthday, I celebrated my life with friends. That same day, 35-year-old Mark Fowler was forbidden to hug or touch anyone because of a no-contact policy for death row inmates at the Oklahoma State Penitentiary. At 9:00 that night, Mark was strapped to a gurney and injected with lethal drugs. He was pronounced dead at 9:07.

Life. Death. Joy. Despair. The lines of our lives crisscross. Touching. Not touching. We are dealing with an invisible world. Fight the invisibility, the namelessness of those who disappear from the charts bearing only prison numbers. Find a way to make it personal.

> ❖ *I guarantee you that if I could set Edward, or any of my clients down in a room with twelve jurors and just leave them there for twenty-four hours, you would never get the death penalty in any case, because they would realize that there is a human element to this guy and they wouldn't do it.*
>
> ~CLIVE STAFFORD SMITH

In a published interview, Michelle Lyons, a young Texas reporter who covers the "execution beat" for the *Huntsville Item*, remembered being a "little bit" bothered by the plight of one prisoner she saw put to death. Her testimony is a stark reminder of just how invisible the people on death row can become:

For some reason, there are memories that just stand out more than others. The one that, lately, has bothered me a little bit . . . I can't even remember the man's name. That's bad. You know, you cover so many of these cases, the names, they kind of start being jumbled together. But what struck me about it was, he was on the gurney, and he just stared at the ceiling the entire time. He never looked at the sides, he never spoke. He just looked at the ceiling and cried. He had no witnesses on his behalf and I thought, you know, that's really lonely. He didn't have friends, relatives, or anybody. Nobody had come. The victim's family was there. At the same time you sympathize with him, but you mostly sympathize with the victim's family, you know.

In Case I'm Murdered

As Shakespeare's play *Cymbeline* comes to an end, one man kneels before another whom he has seriously wronged at the core of the play's action. The repentant man confesses his crime saying, "heavy conscience sinks my knee," fully expecting the punishment of death. But Shakespeare ends this play with redemption for all, and, in this spirit, the wronged man is moved by mercy, not revenge:

> *Kneel not to me.*
> *The power that I have on you is to spare you;*
> *The malice towards you to forgive you. Live,*
> *And deal with others better.*

During the 1993 gubernatorial race in New York State, many voters clamored for the return of the death penalty. In response, a small group of Catholic nuns, priests, and lay people in Brooklyn formed the Cherish Life Circle, a support group for New Yorkers opposing capital punishment from a faith-based perspective. Members of the Circle organized parish study days, wrote articles and homilies, gave speeches, circulated petitions, and talked with politicians about their opposition to the death penalty. They also began conducting annual, ecumenical candlelight services for families of murder victims.

Still, members of the Cherish Life Circle wanted a tool with which to reveal their anti-death penalty position in a nonjudgmental manner, especially to friends and relatives who held different opinions.

One of the group's founders, Mercy Sister Camille D'Arienzo, helped initiate a petition drive using a document called the Declaration of Life. After several statements proclaiming opposition to capital punishment, the petition reads: "Therefore, I hereby declare that, should I die as a result of a violent crime, I request that the person or persons found guilty of homicide for my killing not be subject to or put in jeopardy of the death penalty under any circumstances, no matter how heinous their crime or how much I may have suffered."

Signers are requested to have the document witnessed and nota-
rized, then filed with appropriate papers, such as wills and organ-donor
cards. The idea is that, in the event of a signer's murder, the Declaration will be presented in court as one factor in determining the sentence. This voice from the grave, pleading for mercy, as it were, will not
be a legally binding document, but might function to have an impact on
the sentencing of the convicted.

People willing to sign the Declaration are asked to notify the original Cherish Life Circle so that a record of supporters can be maintained. In exchange for a small donation, a signer receives a wallet card,
attesting to the existence of the Declaration.

In addition to the Cherish Life Circle, other groups circulate the
Declaration of Life, sometimes with slightly altered wording, making it
available by mail or on the Internet, including Catholics Against Capital Punishment, The Friends Committee to Abolish the Death Penalty,
and Unitarian Universalists Against the Death Penalty. To date, the list
of signers is still growing, numbering in the tens of thousands.

Say Their Names—Resist Disappearance

❖ *To become genuinely hungry for justice makes it possible to join with
the poor in a common struggle. It is our own hunger that begins to drive
us, not somebody else's problem.*

*. . . As long as death row inmates, and the poor, are marginalized in
their isolation and we "concerned religious" are paralyzed in our guilt,
no real change is possible. It is the hunger and thirst for justice of which
the Beatitudes speak that could bring us together and transform the social
landscape.*

~BROTHER BERNIE SPITZLEY

Kathleen A. O'Shea is someone who has let the people on death row
get under her skin. A nun for twenty-five years, she fell into working
with women prisoners quite unintentionally, assuming it would be a
short, study-related project. In the epilogue to her book *Women on the
Row: Revelations from Both Sides of the Bars*, she makes it clear that, for
her, these women are no longer an academic project. She knows that
their lives and her own are connected. She writes:

In the past few years, since I began writing about women on death
row, I have been frequently asked, "How did you get this in-

volved? How did you become so passionate about all this?" And up until writing this book I've always said, "It's because I met a woman on death row." Meaning, once I put a face to women on death row I could no longer ignore them. But now, after this, I might say, "It's because I saw my face on a woman on death row." I realized in my first interview with a woman awaiting execution that our similarities were quite substantial, our differences somewhat circumstantial.

In the same book, O'Shea writes that her association with the women awaiting execution has altered her life. In the preface, she describes her reaction to a disturbing E-mail received after the publication of her first book, *Women and the Death Penalty:*

> I received the following E-mail: THEY GET WHAT THEY DESERVE. MAY THEIR NAMES BE ERASED FROM THE BOOK OF LIFE. I keep that quote in front of me to remind me what the women on death row asked me to say about them to the public. Say our names, they told me. These women do not want to be erased from the book of life.

I am reminded, as I end this book, of the long poem-meditation titled "Rest in Peace" written by Frederic and Mary Ann Brussat, and inspired by the Vietnamese Buddhist monk Thich Nhat Hanh in the days immediately following the 9/11 terrorist attack. It was widely circulated on the Internet. In it, the poets speak in the voices of all involved—animate and inanimate—in the first person. Each imagined voice ends with the prayer, "May I rest in peace" or "May I know peace."

In the poem, readers are invited to imagine being a tower "standing tall in the clear blue sky / feeling a violent blow in my side"—"May I rest in peace." We imagine being a pigeon eating crumbs in the plaza when suddenly fire rains from the skies. "May I rest in peace." We imagine being a piece of paper, once on an office desk, now a part of the debris scattered by the wind. "May I rest in peace."

In this sustained meditation, readers imagine the many shapes of the human experience on 9/11—a terrified airline passenger, a firefighter, an office worker who survived by escaping down the stairs. We imagine being a tourist in Times Square, a family member who has just learned of the death of a loved one, a pastor who must comfort others, a store owner who is now out of business, a little boy in New Jersey waiting for his father to come home. "May I know peace."

And the poem eventually includes the imagined first-voice narratives of a United States general, an intelligence officer, and then a terrorist and a terrorist sympathizer. The poem ends with these words:

> *I am a child of God*
> *who believes that we are all children of God*
> *and we are all part of one another.*
> *May we all know peace.*

In the spirit of this poem/meditation, I close with the hope that we will do the work of imagining each other. Let us imagine speaking in the voice of the victim of violent crime and in the voice of the weapon. Speak in the voice of the bloody bed sheet or the back alley, and of the stars in the sky that witnessed the terror of brutality. Speak in the voice of the one who first came upon the violent scene and of the police officers. Speak in the raw, agonized voice of the victim's mother or father, of the victim's spouse, child, or heartbroken best friend, the victim's cat.

Speak the truth in the voice of the emergency-room nurse, the coroner, the court officers, the lawyers, the judge, and the jurors. Add to those, the voices of the journalist and the television reporter, and the janitor who sweeps the courtroom after everyone else has gone home.

In the loving, expansive spirit of Thich Nhat Hanh and the poets he inspired, find the voice of the guilty person on death row, and find the voice of the innocent one. Find the voice of the remorseful one and of the brazen one too bitter or hardened for remorse.

Speak in the voice of the bewildered child left behind by the death row inmate, the aging mother, the devastated younger brother, the betrayed friend, the co-worker, the social worker. Speak in the voice of the first-grade teacher who never imagined that one of her students would wind up on death row.

Find the voice of the prison chaplain who will pray the Lord's Prayer with the condemned, and of the kitchen worker who will prepare the tray of food for the last meal. Find the voice of the one who will tighten the strap on the prisoner's left leg the night of the execution. Give voice to the stark and sterile death chamber and to the syringe.

Speak in the voice of the angry protester who feels vindicated by the execution, the family member who expects it to bring "closure," and in the voice of the vigil-keepers who mourn.

The list can go on and on, and each voice you discover inside yourself will count. We are the human family. We are in this together. We are—whether we like it or not—a part of each other.

Let no one be cast out of the circle. Let no name be erased from the book of life.

Find the voices. Find and cherish all the voices. This is our work. May we all know peace.

> *The quality of mercy is not strained;*
> *It droppeth as the gentle rain from heaven*
> *Upon the place beneath. It is twice blest;*
> *It blesseth him that gives and him that takes.*
> *'Tis mightiest in the mightiest; it becomes*
> *The throned monarch better than his crown;*
> *His sceptre shows the force of temporal power,*
> *The attribute to awe and majesty,*
> *Wherein doth sit the dread and fear of kings;*
> *But mercy is above this sceptred sway,*
> *It is enthroned in the hearts of kings,*
> *It is an attribute to God himself;*
> *And earthly power doth then show likest God's*
> *When mercy seasons justice.*
> ~PORTIA'S SPEECH FROM *THE MERCHANT OF*
> *VENICE* BY WILLIAM SHAKESPEARE

❧ Appendix 1 ❧

Excerpts from Illinois Governor George Ryan's Speech on Commutations, Saturday, January 11, 2003, as published in the *New York Times.*

The other day, I received a call from Nelson Mandela. I was at Manny's having a corned beef sandwich, and I talked to Nelson Mandela for about 20 minutes. The message he basically delivered to me was that the United States sets the example for justice and fairness for the rest of the world. We're not in league with Europe, Canada, Mexico, most of South and Central America. These countries rejected the death penalty. We are partners in death with several third world countries. Did you know even Russia has called a moratorium?

The death penalty has been abolished in 12 states, and in none of these states has the homicide rate increased. Now here's a good number for you to remember: In Illinois last year we had about 1,000 murders, and only 2 percent of that 1,000 were sentenced to death. I want to know, where is the fairness and equality in that? The death penalty in Illinois is not imposed fairly or uniformly because of the absence of standards for 102 counties in this state. State's attorneys decide whether to request the death sentence. Should geography be a factor in determining who gets the death sentence? I don't think it should, but in Illinois it makes a difference. You are five times more likely to get a death sentence for first-degree murder in the rural areas of this state than you are right here in Cook County. Five times more likely. Where is the fairness in this justice system? Where is the proportionality? . . .

I never intended to be an activist on this issue, needless to say. Soon after taking office I watched in surprise and amazement as freed death row inmate Anthony Porter was released from jail. As a free man, he ran into Northwestern University Professor Dave Protess—where's David?—It was a memory I'll never forget, seeing little Anthony Porter run into your arms as a free man. He poured his heart and soul, David did, into proving Porter's innocence with his journalism students.

Anthony Porter was 48 hours away from being wheeled into the execution chamber, where the state would kill him.

It would all be so antiseptic, and most of us would not have even paused, except that Anthony Porter was innocent. He was innocent of the double murder for which he had been condemned to die.

And after Mr. Porter's case there was a report by *Chicago Tribune* reporters Steve Mills and Ken Armstrong that documented the systemic failures of our capital punishment system. And you've all read it. I can't imagine: half, half, if you will, of the nearly 300 capital cases in Illinois had been reversed for a new trial or re-sentencing. How many of you here today who are professionals can get by with 50 percent accuracy?

Thirty-three of the death row inmates were represented at trial by an attorney who had later been disbarred or at some point suspended from the practice of law. Of the more than 160 death row inmates, 35 were African American defendants who had been convicted or condemned to die not by a jury of their peers, but by all-white juries.

More than two-thirds of the inmates on death row were African American.

And 46 inmates were convicted on the basis of testimony from jailhouse informants.

I can recall looking at these cases and the information from the Mills/Armstrong series and I asked myself, and my staff: How does that happen? How in God's name does that happen? In America, how does it happen? I've been asking this question for nearly three years and so far nobody's answered this question.

Then over the next few months, there were three more exonerated men, freed because their sentence hinged on a jailhouse informant, or new DNA technology proved beyond a shadow of a doubt their innocence. . . .

If you really want to know what's outrageous and unconscionable, outrageous and unconscionable, 17 exonerated death row inmates is nothing short of a catastrophic failure. . . .

Our capital system is haunted by the demon of error: error in determining guilt, and error in determining who among the guilty deserves to die. Because of all of these reasons today I am commuting the sentences of all death row inmates.

This is a blanket commutation. I didn't believe I would do it myself. I realize it will draw ridicule, scorn and anger from many who oppose this decision. They'll say that I am usurping the decisions of judges and juries and state legislators. But as I have said, the people of our state have vested in me to act in the interest of justice. Even if the exercise of my power becomes my burden, I'll bear it. Because our Constitution compels it. I sought this office, and even in my final days of holding it I can't shrink from the obligations to justice and fairness that it demands.

There have been many days and many nights where my staff and I have been deprived of sleep in order to conduct the exhaustive review of the system. But I can tell you this: I'm going to sleep well tonight knowing I made the right decision.

ᴁ Appendix 2 ᴂ

Death Row Prayer recited each week at the Church of Gethsemane, 1012 Eighth Avenue, Brooklyn, NY, 11215.

Introduction to Prayer (sometimes read, as background information):

The Church of Gethsemane has a special mission, to create an intentional congregation of neighborhood people, prisoners, ex-prisoners, and their families, and people in solidarity with the poor and the imprisoned.

As an expression of our commitment to create justice and peace in this world, we pray especially for persons on death row. There are now more than 3,500 men, women, and children in prisons across the United States, awaiting death by electrocution, lethal injection, or the gas chamber. The people on death row are both young and old and are members of various ethnic groups.

Through our public prayer, we remind ourselves that killing is wrong and that the death penalty does not end the cycle of violence that distorts our lives—but continues it. By lifting up sixty-seven names each Sunday, in one year's time, we can pray for almost everyone who is now waiting on death row.

Death Row Prayer:

Let us pray together: Merciful God, the names we lift before you are persons whom society has declared expendable, worthless, and useless. We do not know their life's stories, nor do we know why they are on death row. We do know, however, that all human beings have worth and that killing is unjust, betraying our deepest values about human life. Be with each of these persons, during their darkest hour, and grant that this society and this world will end these senseless and merciless executions. The people we pray for today are on death row in *(name of state)*.

(Read list of names.) Amen.

❧ Sources ❧

Chapter 1: The Sad and Sordid History of Capital Punishment

BOOKS / PAMPHLETS

Among the Lowest of the Dead: The Culture of Death Row, David Von Drehle, NY, Times Books, Random House, 1995, p. 122

Bryan, Robert R., "The Defender" in *A Punishment in Search of a Crime: Americans Speak Out against the Death Penalty*, Ian Gray and Moira Stanley, eds., Avon Books, 1989

Crime and Punishment in American History, Lawrence M. Friedman, BasicBooks, 1993

Dead Man Walking: An Eyewitness Account of the Death Penalty in the United States, Helen Prejean, C.S.J., Random House, 1993

Death Penalty: An American History, Stuart Banner, Harvard University Press, 2002

Death Work: A Study of the Modern Execution Process, Robert Johnson, Wadsworth Publishing Co, 1990

Dow, David R., "How the Death Penalty Really Works," in *Machinery of Death: The Reality of America's Death Penalty Regime*, David R. Dow and Mark Dow, eds, Routledge, 2002

Execution Protocol: Inside America's Capital Punishment Industry, Stephen Trombley, Crown Publishers, 1992

Facing the Death Penalty: Essays on a Cruel and Unusual Punishment, Michael L. Radelet, ed., Temple University Press, 1989

Hard Time Blues, Sasha Abramsky, St. Martin's Press, 2002

Holy Bible, New Revised Standard Version, Thomas Nelson Publishers, 1989

Lesson before Dying, Ernest J. Gaines, Vintage Books, Random House, 1993

Live from Death Row, Mumia Abu-Jamal, Addison-Wesley Publishing Co, 1995

Never-Ending Wrong, Katherine Anne Porter, Little, Brown and Co., 1977

Pictures at an Execution: An Inquiry into the Subject of Murder, Wendy Lesser, Harvard University Press, 1993

Prisons that Could Not Hold, Barbara Deming, Spinsters Ink, 1985

Punishment and the Death Penalty: The Current Debate, Robert M. Baird and Stuart E. Rosenbaum, eds., Prometheus Books, 1995

This River of Courage: Generations of Women's Resistance and Action, Pam McAllister, New Society Publishers, 1991

When the State Kills: Capital Punishment and the American Condition, Austin Sarat, Princeton University Press, 2001

Who Owns Death? Capital Punishment, the American Conscience, and the End of Executions, Robert Jay Lifton and Greg Mitchell, HarperCollins Publishers, Inc., 2000

Woman Hating, Andrea Dworkin, E. P. Dutton, 1974

NEWSPAPERS AND MAGAZINES

New Yorker, July 30, 2001, "Slice of Life: How a Convicted Killer's Corpse Brought Anatomy into the Digital Age," Gordon Grice

New York Times, May 13, 2001, "Europe's View of the Death Penalty," Editorial

New York Times, September 9, 2001, "Chinese Fight Crime with Torture and Executions," Craig S. Smith

New York Times, May 17, 2002, "In Pakistan, Rape Victims Are the 'Criminals'," Seth Mydans

New York Times, June 30, 2002, "Secrecy of Japan's Executions Is Criticized as Unduly Cruel," Howard W. French

New York Times, January 6, 2003, "As Stoning Case Proceeds, Nigeria Stands Trial," Somini Sengupta

New York Times Magazine, January 27, 2002, "This Woman Has Been Sentenced to Death by Stoning," Richard Dowden

ONLINE RESOURCES

"Death Penalty Facts: International Human Rights Standards," Amnesty International: Program to Abolish the Death Penalty—*www.amnestyusa.org/abolish/international_h_r_standards.html*

Dieter, Richard C. (executive director, DPIC), "International Perspectives on the Death Penalty: A Costly Isolation for the U.S.," Death Penalty Information Center, October 1999—*www.deathpenaltyinfo.org/internationalreport.html*

France-Presse, Agence, "Executions More than Doubled Worldwide Last Year Group Says," the *Nando Times*, June 28, 2002—*www.nandotimes.com/world/story/450670p-3605099c.html*

Johnson, Britt, "Biblical Traditions and the Death Penalty," The Other Side online, *www.theotherside.org/resources/dp/biblical_traditions.html*

"Pakistan Mob Stones Man to Death for Blasphemy," Reuters, July 5, 2002

OTHER RESOURCES

Cliff Frasier, "Epiphany Sunday Sermon," delivered at the Church of Gethsemane, Brooklyn, NY, January 5, 2003

Chapter 2: Three Myths about the Death Penalty

BOOKS / PAMPHLETS

Among the Lowest of the Dead, David Von Drehle, Bedau, Hugo, Essay 26 in *Congregation of the Condemned: Voices against the Death Penalty*, Shirley Dicks, ed., Prometheus Books, 1991

Bryan, Robert R., in *A Punishment in Search of a Crime*

Choosing Mercy: A Mother of Murder Victims Pleads to End the Death Penalty, Antoinette Bosco, Orbis Books, 2001

Dead Wrong: A Death Row Lawyer Speaks Out Against Capital Punishment, Michael A. Mello, University of Wisconsin Press, 1997

Legal Lynching: The Death Penalty and America's Future, Rev. Jesse L. Jackson, Sr., Representative Jesse L. Jackson, Jr., and Bruce Shapiro, The New Press, 2001

Slow Coming Dark: Interviews on Death Row, Doug Magee, Pilgrim Press, 1980

Stafford-Smith, Clive, "Killing the Death Penalty with Kindness," in *Machinery of Death*

Who Owns Death? Lifton and Mitchell

NEWSPAPERS AND MAGAZINES

CACP News Notes, Catholics against Capital Punishment, (Arlington, VA), July 20, 1998, "Are We Hungry Enough?" Brother Bernie Spitzley, SVD

Nation, January 8, 2001, "Death Trip: The American Way of Execution," Robert Sherrill

New York Times, March 6, 2003, "A Sharply Divided Supreme Court Upholds the 'Three-Strikes' Law in California"

San Francisco Examiner, February 7, 1999, "Some forgive the killers of loved ones"

Texas Observer, October 10, 1997, "The Execution Machine: Texas Death Row," Steven G. Kellman

ONLINE RESOURCES

Cullen, Dave, "The Reluctant Activist," Salon News, October 15, 1999—*www.salon.com/news/feature/1999/10/15/laramie*

"Death Penalty Facts: Deterrence," Amnesty International: Program to Abolish the Death Penalty—*www.amnestyusa.org/abolish/deterrence.html*

"Does Revenge Bring Closure?" Fight the Death Penalty in USA—*www.fdp.dk/uk/closure.htm*

"James Byrd, Jr." Power of 1—*www.powerof1.org/byrd.html*

"Jasper: On the Trail of James Byrd, Jr. (from the journals of H. Palmer Hall),"—*http://library.stmarytx.edu/pgpress/jamesbyrdjr.html*

Larson, Nancy, "Matthew's Mom Has a Vision," Vital Voice, October 6, 2001—*www.thevitalvoice.com/2001_1026/Matthews_Mom.html*

"Mathew Shepard International: A Resource Guide"—*www.worldzone.net/international/mattshepard*

"Seven Steps from Misery Justice to Social Transformation," Ruth Morris, *Coalition for the Abolition of Prisons Newsletter*, June 1999—*www. noprisons.org*

"Southern Regions Historically Have Had Higher Homicide Rates than other Regions," U.S. Department of Justice, Bureau of Justice Statistics—*www.ojp.usdoj.gov/bjs/homicide/region.htm*

Tariq Khamisa Foundation— *www.tkf.org.*

"Victim's Son Holds Prayer for Killer," The Associated Press, July 4, 2002

"Welcome to Huntsville!? Texas and the Death Penalty"—*http://members.aol.com/gabi20uhl/Page7b.html*

Chapter 3: Finding Common Ground

BOOKS / PAMPHLETS

Armbrust, Shawn, "Chance and the Exoneration of Anthony Porter," in *Machinery of Death*

Actual Innocence: Five Days to Execution, and Other Dispatches from the Wrongly Convicted, Barry Scheck, Peter Neufeld, Jim Dwyer, Doubleday, 2000

Bright, Stephen B., (Director, Southern Center for Human Rights, Atlanta), "Discrimination, Death, and Denial: Race and the Death Penalty," in *Machinery of Death*

Dead Wrong, Michael A. Mello

Dow, David R., "How the Death Penalty Really Works," in *Machinery of Death*

Executed God: The Way of the Cross in Lockdown America, Mark Lewis Taylor, Fortress Press, 2001

Far Away, Caryl Churchill, Theatre Communications Group, 2001

Going Up the River: Travels in a Prison Nation, Joseph T. Hallinan, Random House, 2001

In Spite of Innocence: The Ordeal of 400 Americans Wrongly Convicted of Crimes Punishable by Death, Michael L. Radelet, Hugo Adam Bedau, Constance E. Putnam, Northeastern University Press, 1992

Last Rights: 13 Fatal Encounters with the State's Justice, Joseph B. Ingle, Abingdon Press, 1990

Legal Lynching, Jackson, et al

Stafford-Smith, Clive, "An Englishman Abroad," in *A Punishment in Search of a Crime: Americans Speak out against the Death Penalty*

NEWSPAPERS AND MAGAZINES

Amnesty International Report, May, 1999, "Killing with Prejudice: Race and Death Penalty in the USA," (no byline)

Atlanta Journal, November 7, 2000, "Questions Are Raised after an Inmate Is Force-fed Medication," Rhonda Cook

Austin Chronicle, January 21, 2000, "Executing Justice," Erica C. Barnett

CACP News Notes, September 28, 1997, "Address to the New York State Association of Criminal Defense Lawyers, Supreme Court Justice William Brennan, 1990"

Christianity and Crisis, February 5, 1990, "Casting the First Stone: Capital Punishment is still a Moral Problem," Lloyd Steffen

Justice Jottings: Program Guide for Criminal Justice Sunday, February 11, 1990, "Toward Nonviolence: Abolishing the Death Penalty," Presbyterian Criminal Justice Program

Justicia, September–October, 2000, "The Mentally Ill and the Criminal Justice System," Clare Regan

Justicia, November–December, 2000, "Reducing Racial Disparity in the Criminal Justice System: A Sentencing Project Report—Review," Clare Regan

Mother Jones, December 23, 1999, "Wasted Youth," Vince Beiser

Nation, April 7, 1997, "Law and Order: Sleeping Lawyer Syndrome," Bruce Shapiro

New York Times, February 5, 1999, "Class of Sleuths to Rescue on Death Row: Journalism Students Track Down Suspect after Re-enacting Killing," Pam Belluck

New York Times, May 29, 2002, "In Similar Cases, One Inmate Is Executed, One Wins Stay," Sara Rimer

New York Times, June 4, 2002, "Inmate Whose Lawyer Slept Gets New Trial," Linda Greenhouse

New York Times, June 21, 2002, "Citing 'National Consensus,' Justices Bar Death Penalty for Retarded Defendants," Linda Greenhouse

New York Times, November 3, 2002, "Seeking Death Penalty, U.S. May Let Virginia Try 2 First," Eric Lichtblau

New York Times, January 5, 2003, "Prosecutors' Morbid Neckties Stir Criticism," Jeffrey Gettleman

New York Times, January 8, 2003, "Death Penalty Found More Likely if Victim Is White," Adam Liptak

New York Times, January 12 2003, "Citing Issue of Fairness, Governor Clears Out Death Row in Illinois," Jodi Wilgoren

New York Times, January 28, 2003, "Justices Deny Inmate Appeal in Execution of Juveniles," Linda Greenhouse

New York Times, March 16, 2003, "Condemned Killer Exposed to Nerve Gas Seeks Mercy," Adam Liptak

New York Times, March 24, 2003, "Longtime Death Case Lawyer Appeals Ouster," Adam Liptak

New York Times, April 24, 2003, "Pull the Plug," Bob Herbert

Nonviolent Activist, July–August, 2002, "Abolishing the Death Penalty: Not if but When," Steven W. Hawkins (Executive Director, National Coalition to Abolish the Death Penalty)

Other Side, November–December, 2000, "The End of Innocence," Philip Brasfield

Press (Atlantic City, NJ), April 6, 2000, "Death Penalty, Like other Government Programs, Is Rife with Error," George Will

ONLINE RESOURCES

"Betty Lou Beets Executed in Texas," Reuters, February 24, 2000

Carrillo, Silvio, "Can Violent Criminals Be Too Young to Execute?" SpeakOut .com, May 3, 2000—*http://speakout.com/activism/issue_briefs/1165b-1.html*

Colb, Sherry F., "Medicating Prisoners for Execution: A Ruling Raises more Questions," CNN.com Law Center—*www.cnn.com/2003/LAW/02/27/findlaw. analysis.colb.drugs.execution/*

Da Costa-Fernandes, Manuela, "Manny Babbitt Laid to Rest," SouthCoast Today, May 11, 1999—*www.s-t.com/daily/05-99/05-11-99/a0110011.htm*

Dawkins, Christine, "Overcoming Murder with Murder," *Bearing Witness: The on-line magazine of spirituality-based social action and peacemaking*, February 8, 2002— *www.bearingwitnessjournal.com/reverence/deathpenalty.html*

"Death Penalty," Human Rights Watch World Report 2003: United States— *www.hrw.org/wr2k3/us.html*

"Death Penalty Facts: Arbitrary and Unfair Proceedings," Amnesty International: Program to Abolish the Death Penalty—*www.amnestyusa.org/abolish/arbitrary andunfair.html*

"Death Penalty Facts: Juveniles," Amnesty International: Program to Abolish the Death Penalty—*www.amnestyusa.org/abolish/juveniles.html*

"Death Penalty Facts: Mental Illness," Amnesty International: Program to Abolish the Death Penalty—*www.amnestyusa.org/abolish/mental_illness.html*

"Death Penalty Facts: Racial Prejudices," Amnesty International: Program to Abolish the Death Penalty—*www.amnestyusa.org/abolish/racialprejudices.html*

"The Execution of Louis Jones," *Talk Left: The Politics of Crime*, March 18, 2003— *www.talkleft.com/archives/002647.html*

"Five Reasons to Oppose the Death Penalty," Campaign to End the Death Penalty—*www.nodeathpenalty.org/fiveRs1.html*

"Killing with Prejudice: Race and Death Penalty in the USA," Amnesty International, 1999—*www.amnestyusa.org/rightsforall/dp/race/summary.html*

"Seven Myths which Support the Death Penalty,"—*www.netpath.net/~ucch/pfadp/*

Wilton, Charles, "Innocence is Irrelevant," *Peacework* magazine, April, 1999— *www.afsc.org/pwork/0499/049906.htm*

Chapter 4: Facing Complicated Truths

BOOKS

Bruck, David (capital defense lawyer, Columbia, SC), "Banality of Evil," in *A Punishment in Search of a Crime*

Choosing Mercy, Antoinette Bosco, Orbis Books, 2001

Cuomo, Mario M., "Eye for an Eye—Injustice," in *World Without Violence: Can Gandhi's Vision Become Reality?* Arun Gandhi, ed., Wiley Eastern Limited, 1994

Deming, Barbara, "Remembering Who We Are," in *We Are All Part of One Another: A Barbara Deming Reader*, Jane Meyerding, ed., New Society Publishers, 1984

Executed God: The Way of the Cross in Lockdown America, Mark Lewis Taylor, Fortress, 2001

Forgiving the Dead Man Walking, Debbie Morris with Gregg Lewis, Zondervan Publishing House, 1998

Keve, Paul,(former prison administrator, author, professor in the field of corrections and criminal justice), "Virginia Is for Lovers," in *A Punishment in Search of a Crime*

Pieces of My Mind, Andrew A. Rooney, Atheneum, 1984

Stafford-Smith, Clive, in *A Punishment in Search of a Crime*

NEWSPAPERS AND MAGAZINES

CACP News Notes, Catholics Against Capital Punishment, (Arlington, VA), June 12, 1998, "Don't Let Those Who Murder Turn *Us* to Murder," Excerpts from remarks by State Representatives Clifton C. Below and Robert R. Cushing

CACP News Notes, Catholics Against Capital Punishment, July 20, 1998, "Are We Hungry Enough?" Br. Bernie Spitzley, SVD

Friends Journal, April, 1990, "The Model of the Thief," Alfred A. Gobell

New York Times, February 8, 1998, "Dead Women Waiting: Who's Who on Death Row," Sam Howe Verhovek

San Francisco Chronicle, September 11, 2002, "Author on Death Row Loses Appeal: Judges Suggest Clemency by Governor for Killer Nominated for Nobel Prize," Bob Egelko

ONLINE RESOURCES

"Costs of the Death Penalty," *www.deathpenaltyinfo.org/article.php?did=108&
scid=7*
"Karla's Execution Day"—*http://members.tripod.com/Mia_3/kTucker.html*
"Letter of Karla Faye Tucker"—*http://agitator.com/dp/98/karlaletter.html*
"Millions to Kill—Pennies to Heal," National Coalition to Abolish the Death
Penalty—*www.ncadp.org//html/fact3.html*
"On Death Row, an Author and Nobel Nominee," Paul Van Slambrouck—
www.streetgangs.com/topics/2000/112800tookie.html
"Stephen Wayne Anderson"—*www.clarkprosecutor.org/html/death/US/anderson
754.htm*
"Stephen Anderson's Poetry"—*www.deathpenalty.org/facts/cases/anderson_poetry.shtml*

OTHER SOURCES

David Dyson, Pastor of the Lafayette Presbyterian Church, Brooklyn, NY, personal
correspondence
Denise Gragg, Orange County public defender, quoted in *CACP News Notes, Catho-
lics against Capital Punishment*, Arlington, VA, vol. 7. no. 3, 7/20/98
Rabbi Alan Lew, excerpt from his message given near the gates of San Quentin
State Prison, at the vigil to mark the execution of Young Elk, Darrell Rich.

Chapter 5: Varieties of Nonviolent Action

BOOKS / PAMPHLETS

Death Penalty: A Guide for Christians, Bob Gross, FaithQuest, 1991
Executed God, Mark Lewis Taylor
Green Mile, Stephen King, Pocket Books/Simon & Schuster, 1996
Gross, Bob, "Discussion Guide for the Film/Video *Dead Man Walking*," Criminal
Justice Program, Presbyterian Church-U.S.A. Available on-line by *The Other
Side* (*http://www.theotherside.org/resources/dp/dmw_guide.html*)
Heart Politics, Fran Peavey, New Society Publishers, 1986
Let the Children March: The Children's Crusade, August 18–20, 1997, Compiled by the
Children of the Crusade, Plough Publishing House, 1997
McReynolds, David, "A Philosophy of Nonviolence," A. J. Muste Memorial Insti-
tute Essay Series #15, 2000
Obedience to Authority: An Experimental View, Stanley Milgram, Harper Colophon
Books, 1974
The Politics of Nonviolent Action: Part Two—The Methods of Nonviolent Action, Gene
Sharp, Porter Sargent Publishers, 1973

NEWSPAPERS AND MAGAZINES

CACP News Notes, December 31, 1998, "US Bishops' Statement, Pope's Comments
Kindle Hopes for Stronger Church-based Actions against Death Penalty," (no
byline)

Catholic Radical, October–November, 1997, "Children against Executions," Clare Schaeffer-Duffy, Justin Duffy

Endeavor: Live Voices from Death Row, February–May, 1990, "Whosoever Is without Sin," Betty Lou Beets #810

Endeavor: Live Voices from Death Row, February–May, 1990, "Boycott," Robert West #731

Mother Jones, "Undercutting Executions," Justine Sharrock, December, 28, 2001

New York Times, May 18, 2003, "Steadfast Witnesses to Deaths Far Off," Anemona Hartocollis

Nonviolent Activist, October–November, 1991,"Refusing to Pay for the Death Penalty," David Nuttall

Nonviolent Activist, September–October, 1999, "How Freedom Rang: On Civil Disobedience, Coalitions and Mumia Abu-Jamal," Matt Meyer

Nonviolent Activist, July–August, 2002, "Abolishing the Death Penalty: Not *If* but *When*," Steven W. Hawkins

NYADP NEWS, Spring, 2003, "Voices for a New Justice Tour," Jon S. Rice

Other Side, September–December, 1997, "Practical Actions against Capital Punishment: On Staying True to God in a Killing Culture," Mark William Olson

Other Side, September–December, 1997, "Uprooting the Seeds of Violence," Rev. Bernice A. King

Sojourners magazine, May–June, 1996, "Hearing the Facts about the Death Penalty," Julie Polter

ONLINE RESOURCES

"Abolition Day," Citizens United for Alternatives to the Death Penalty— *www.cuadp.org/samplepr.html*

Abolition Wear— Citizens United for Alternatives to the Death Penalty *www.cuadp-.org/abolitionwear.html*

Abolitionist Action Committee—*www. abolition.org*

Abolitionist Action Committee of Pax Christi USA—*www.abolition.org/pax_christi_usa.html*

American Friends Service Committee—*www.afsc.org*

Amnesty International: AIKIDS—(simplified letter-writing guide for children) *www.amnestyusa.org/aikids/writing_guide.html*

Amnesty International: Urgent Action Network—*www.amnestyusa.org/urgent*

Campaign for Criminal Justice Reform—*www.CJReform.org*

Campaign to End the Death Penalty—*www.nodeathpenalty.org*

Catholics Against Capital Punishment—*www.cacp.org*

Catholic Worker—*www.catholicworker.org*

Chavis, Melody Ermachild, "Death Penalty Pilgrimage," *www.prisonwall.org/dpart.htm*

Citizens for a Moratorium on Federal Executions—*www.federalmoratorium.org*

Citizens United for Alternatives to the Death Penalty (CUADP)—*www.cuadp.org*

Clergy Coalition to End Executions—*www.clergycoalition.org*

Critical Resistance—*www.critical resistance.org*

Davidson, Douglas, "Choosing Life: Four Activists from Different Religious Traditions Share Thoughts on the Challenges of Organizing against the Death Penalty," Death Penalty Religious—*www.deathpenaltyreligious.org/action/ongoing/choosinglife.html*

Death Penalty Focus—*www.deathpenalty.org*

Death Penalty Information Center—*www.deathpenaltyinfo.org*

Erickson, Arnold, "The Night of an Execution," *www.prisonwall.org/vigil.htm*

Fellowship of Reconciliation—*www.forusa.org*

"Fifth Annual National Weekend of Faith in Action on the Death Penalty," Amnesty International report, October 11–13, 2002—*www.amnestyusa.org/events/nwfa 1011–132002.html*

Fight the Death Penalty in USA—*www.fdp.dk/uk/strategy.htm*

Floridians for Alternatives to the Death Penalty—*www.fadp.org*

Hammel, Andrew, "The Anti-Death Penalty Movement Has Failed," available from Fight the Death Penalty in USA—*www.fdp.dk/uk/strategy.htm*

Kansas Coalition Against the Death Penalty—*www.kscadp.org*

Lay-Dorsey, Patricia, "Windchime Walker's Journal 24 Archive: 1/25–2/24/02"—*www.windchimewalker.net*

Living Theatre—*www.livingtheatre.org*

Moratorium Campaign—*http:// www.moratoriumcampaign.org.*

Murder Victims' Families for Reconciliation—*www.mvfr.org*

National Coalition to Abolish the Death Penalty—*www.ncadp.org*

New Abolitionist: Newsletter of the Campaign to End the Death Penalty—*www.nodeathpenalty.org*

New Jerseyans for a Death Penalty Moratorium—*www.njmoratorium.org*

New Mexico Coalition to Repeal the Death Penalty—*www.nmrepeal.com*

"News from the struggle to Free Mumia!" compiled by Refuse & Resist!—*www.refuseandresist.org/mumia/actions10.html*

New Yorkers Against the Death Penalty—*www.nyadp.org*

Ohioans to Stop Executions —*www.otse.org*

Oklahoma Coalition to Abolish the Death Penalty—*www.ocadp.org*

Pennsylvania Abolitionists United Against the Death Penalty—*www.pa-abolitionists.org*

People of Faith Against the Death Penalty (North Carolina)—*www.pfadp.org*

Prejean (Sister Helen), "Report from the Front"—*www.prejean.org*

"Prayer Service at Time of Execution" (Vigil Service Models)—*www.richmonduu.org/vpof/service.htm*

Prison Legal News—*www.prisonlegalnews.org*

Project Hope to Abolish the Death Penalty (Alabama)—*www.phadp.org*

Religious Organizing against the Death Penalty—*www.deathpenaltyreligious.org*

Richmond, Ben, "Friends Share Their Faith in Prison," September, 2000, Friends United Meeting—*www.fum.org/QL/issues/0009/friends_share.htm*

Rick Halperin's Death Penalty News—*http://venus.soci.niu.edu/~archives/ABOLISH/rick-halperin*

Texas Coalition to Abolish the Death Penalty—*www.tcadp.org*

"The Texas Killing Machine Targets Canadian Stanley Faulder," David Walsh, World Socialist Web Site, December 10, 1998—*www.wsws.org*

Virginians for Alternatives to the Death Penalty—*www.vadp.org*

OTHER SOURCES

Address: "Message Supporting the Moratorium on the Death Penalty," April 9, 1999, His Holiness the Dalai Lama (Source: *Envisioning, Religious Organizing against the Death Penalty Project*)
Address: "Changing the Nature of Contemporary Death Penalty Debates," Germany, May 22, 2000, Michael L. Radelet, Professor of Sociology at the University of Florida in Lunen
Address given near the gates of San Quentin State Prison at a vigil to mark the execution of Young Elk, Darrell Rich, March 14–15, 2000, Rabbi Alan Lew (author of *One God Clapping: The Spiritual Path of a Zen Rabbi*)
Video, "Children's Crusade to Death Row, August 18–20, 1997," Plough Publishing, Rt. 381 North, Farmington, PA 15437

Chapter 6: Let It Get Under Your Skin

BOOKS / PAMPHLETS

Dead Wrong, Michael A. Mello
Stafford-Smith, Clive, in *A Punishment in Search of a Crime*
Women on the Row: Revelations from Both Sides of the Bars, Kathleen A. O'Shea, Firebrand Books, 2000

NEWSPAPERS AND MAGAZINES

CACP News Notes, Catholics Against Capital Punishment, (Arlington, VA), July 20, 1998, "Are We Hungry Enough?" Br. Bernie Spitzley, SVD
New York Review of Books, August 9, 2001, "Witness to Executions," Sylvie Kauffmann

ONLINE RESOURCES

"Mark Fowler," Oklahoma Coalition to Abolish the Death Penalty—*www.ocadp.org/mark_fowler_clemency.htm*

OTHER SOURCES

Cherish Life Circle / c/o Convent of Mercy, 273 Willoughby Avenue, Brooklyn, NY 11205–1487
David Dyson, pastor of the Lafayette Avenue Presbyterian Church, Brooklyn, NY, Personal correspondence
"Rest in Peace," poem by Frederic and Mary Ann Brussat

❧ INDEX ❧